HEARTBEATS OF HOLINESS

A. Wingrove Taylor

SCHMUL PUBLISHING COMPANY
NICHOLASVILLE, KENTUCKY

COPYRIGHT © 2020 BY SCHMUL PUBLISHING CO.
All rights reserved. No part of this publication may be reproduced or used in any form or by any means—graphic, electronic, or mechanical, including photocopying, recording, taping, or information storage or retrieval systems—without prior written permission of the publishers.

Churches and other noncommercial interests may reproduce portions of this book without prior written permission of the publisher, provided such quotations are not offered for sale—or other compensation in any form—whether alone or as part of another publication, and provided that the text does not exceed 500 words or five percent of the entire book, whichever is less, and does not include material quoted from another publisher. When reproducing text from this book, the following credit line must be included: "From *Heartbeats of Holiness* by A. Wingrove Taylor, © 2020 by Schmul Publishing Co., Nicholasville, Kentucky. Used by permission."

Cover image copyright: <a href="https://www.123rf.com/profile_neirfy">neirfy / 123RF Stock Photo</a>. Used by permission.

Published by Schmul Publishing Co.
PO Box 776
Nicholasville, KY 40340
USA

ISBN 10: 0-88019-632-7
ISBN 13: 978-0-88019-632-1

Visit us on the Internet at www.wesleyanbooks.com, or order direct from the publisher by calling 800-772-6657, or by writing to the above address.

Contents

Foreword/5

1
Birthing—A Holiness Heartbeat/9
Introduction/11
1.1—The Scriptural Beginning in Holiness/15
1.2—A Special Bestowal by Heaven/19
1.3—Spiritual Beloveds at Home/27
1.4—Subsequent Bearing of Harvest/39
1.5—Conclusion/41

2
Burying—A Holiness Heartbeat/43
Introduction/45
2.1—The Scriptures Depict Burying/47
2.2—Sin Demands Burying/51
2.3—Spousal Life Defends Burying/59
2.4—Conclusion/65

3
Belonging—A Holiness Heartbeat/67
Introduction/69
3.1—The Basis of Belonging/71
3.2—The Boundaries of Belonging/79
3.3—The Blessedness of Belonging/87
3.4—Conclusion/93

4
Blessing—A Holiness Heartbeat/95
Introduction/97
4.1—A Hearty Assurance/99
4.2—Heavenly Affections/111
4.3—Holy Authority/115
4.4—The High Almighty/121
4.5—Conclusion/127

5
Becoming—A Holiness Heartbeat/129
Introduction/131
5.1—Paradoxical Truth/133
5.2—Theological Truth/141
5.3—Practical Truth/151
5.4—Conclusion/159

Foreword

THE SERMONS CONTAINED in this book were developed for and preached at God's Bible School and College's annual Campmeeting by Dr. A. Wingrove Taylor. Dr. Taylor was known as God's Bible School's "Favorite Son" and was an annual featured speaker at the Campmeeting for almost 40 years. His influence on GBS Alumni and Campmeeting attendees was profound. It is equally true that his global influence within the holiness tradition was as remarkable as any within the last fifty years. However, since age and illness removed him from active ministry well over a decade ago, I think it is important to give the reader a little biographical information on this most amazing man.

He was born Alarick Wingrove Taylor in 1923 on the Island of Nevis, British West Indies, to Richard Alfred and Irene (Blyden) Taylor, both GBS alumni and both ministers and pioneer missionaries of the then Pilgrim Holiness Church. As a young man, Dr. Taylor described himself as a rebellious boy who longed for the far country. However, in February of 1947, he had a marvelous conversion that changed the trajectory of his life forever. In recounting the story of his conversion, he told of struggling greatly to yield to God—but the yielding came. He then told of struggling to know he was saved. He said, "I wearied myself to the point of exhaustion. Finally, I just fell into bed and went sound asleep. When I awoke the next morning, I had the bright assurance of salvation."

In the fall of 1948, Wingrove enrolled in the Christian Workers Course at GBS, but eventually moved to the college where he completed two diplomas in music, a Bachelor of Theology degree, and a Bachelor of Arts degree. He graduated summa cum laude and valedictorian of his class in 1953. His days at GBS had a profound influence on him. He often said, "This school has been the greatest influence on my life, second only to family and church."

After graduation, he went back to the Island of St. Kitts where Doreen Harper had been waiting for him. They married in 1953 and set out for the Island of Trinidad to pastor for the Pilgrim Holiness Church. It was here that the four Taylor children (Brainerd, Paula, Mary Grace and Phoebe) were born.

Dr. Taylor was quickly recognized for his preaching ability and leadership qualities. This catapulted him into various positions of prominence in the church and other religious organizations. In over fifty years of active ministry throughout the Caribbean he served as a pastor, District Superintendent, College President, Field Superintendent and finally as the General Superintendent of the Wesleyan Holiness Church in the Caribbean. During that time he also served the Wesleyan World Fellowship, the Caribbean Association of Bible Colleges, the Caribbean Evangelical Theological Association, the Evangelical Association of the Caribbean, as Co-chair of the Congress on the Evangelization of the Caribbean, the Director of Lighthouse Literature, and as the Chairman of

Wycliffe Bible Translators of the Caribbean. Internationally, he ministered in forty-three different countries, served on the God's Bible School and College Board of Trustees (forty-four years), and traveled all over the United States as an evangelist, campmeeting speaker and Bible teacher.

Along the way he was honored with four honorary doctorates (Houghton College, Southern Wesleyan University, Caribbean Graduate School of Theology and God's Bible School and College); was named Holiness Exponent of the Year by the Christian Holiness Association; given the Lifetime Achievement Award by Wesleyan Theological Society; and given the Distinguished Alumnus Award from his Alma Mater, God's Bible School and College.

From a simply personal evaluation, Dr. Taylor was a remarkably gifted man. He was a musician, singer, scholar, author, preacher, and administrator. He was peerless; he was fearless; he was orderly (he once told me that next to his Bible, *Robert's Rules of Order* was his most treasured book); he was saintly; he was professional; he was careful; he was logical; he was Biblical; he was sensitive; he was sensible; he was authentic. One of the most remarkable things about Dr. Taylor was that he never stopped growing in his faith and gaining new insight into the Christian life. In 1992, he experienced something that was to change him profoundly. He states it like this:

> I came to a place of excruciating agony and bewilderment about what appeared to be new religious directions all around me. It was then that God steadied and settled me by revealing that the bottom line of Christianity was not merely religion, nor ritual, nor even righteousness, but basically radical relationship with Him. Since then life in Christ, for me, has taken on new peace, purity, poise, power, and freedom. I am now having a richer relationship with oth-

ers because of the precious paradox of exclusive relationship to God and with Him.

As a preacher, Dr. Taylor was a homilist without peer. He had mastered the art of alliteration to the point that every sermon had rhythm and rhyme. Yet at the same time he never sacrificed "sense for sound." This was all done in the context of careful accurate exegesis of the Biblical passage.

On a very personal note, the greatest gift that Wingrove Taylor gave to all of us is not what he has *done* in ministry, but what he *became* while doing ministry. In a world of shallow, image-manipulating, politician preachers— he was the real deal. He personally found and lived out Radical Relationship with Jesus.

—MICHAEL AVERY
*Chancellor, God's Bible
School and College*

1
BIRTHING
A Holiness Heartbeat

"Be ye holy; for I am holy."

"Wherefore gird up the loins of your mind, be sober, and hope to the end for the grace that is to be brought unto you at the revelation of Jesus Christ; as obedient children, not fashioning yourselves according to the former lusts in your ignorance: but as he which hath called you is holy, so be ye holy in all manner of conversation; because it is written, Be ye holy; for I am holy." —*1 Peter 1:13-16*

Introduction

A PHYSICAL HEARTBEAT is the continuous, dynamic contraction of the lower heart chambers that forces blood throughout one's entire body. Physical heartbeats are always necessary to natural life. Similarly, the biblical heartbeats of holiness are absolutely essential to spiritual life in Christ. Holiness is primal. It may be called the central attribute of God, because "I am holy" is the first character statement God made of Himself (Leviticus 11:44).

Holiness is essential. 1 Peter 1:16 reveals that without holiness none can share God's life. 1 Peter 1:15 records that without holiness none can show forth God's likeness; whereas Hebrews 12:14 reaffirms that without holiness "no man shall see the Lord" — that is, be with, dwell with, or enjoy God. It should not be surprising, then, that holiness is universa1. It is God's purpose that all of the beings that He created in His image should be holy (1 Peter 1:16).

Holiness is therefore not confined to certain religious groups or movements. It is not denominational but global. Holiness is also normal. It is not light to fear. It is a life most dear. It is to the spirit what health is to the body, and there are some specific heartbeats or experiences that are essential to the possession of holiness.

Across many years I have had a degree of painful search to come to a sense of thorough establishment on the solid rock of holiness. In practice, my searching led me to birthing (in 1947), to blessing (three years later, 1950), to burying (nine years later, 1959) to becoming (seven years later, 1966); and only from 1992 (twenty-six years later) did I begin really to understand the principle and place of belonging, some forty-five years after birthing. From my experience and increasing study, I am persuaded that these are the heartbeats of holiness.

My order was, of course, sadly mixed up. The true order is rather: birthing, burying, belonging, blessing and becoming. The great need is that all of these essentials of holiness should totally, if not timely, be operative in all of our lives. Holiness comes by comprehension: crisis in gaining, and by comprehension and continuation in growth. I have the conviction that for persons like me, God in His mercy must be more concerned about the necessity of experiencing the organized completeness of holiness data than about the desirability of the ordered crises or continuity of holiness dates. We need not to uproot the past but to upgrade the present.

"Birthing" is the name that we are giving to the first holiness heartbeat. Technically, birthing is the process of giving birth to a child, especially by the use of natural childbirth methods. We are employing "birthing" to refer to spiritual birth, what the Bible speaks of as being "born again" (John 3:3; 1 Peter 1:23).

Many persons in the holiness movement think of holiness or sanctification in terms of what God does for the believer in what we call the second work of grace. To be more accurate, we should speak of the second work of grace as the second crisis work of grace. While there are two crisis works of grace, there are, in relation to holiness, more than two works of grace. There is, for example, the grace of provisional holiness. In contrast to personal holiness, provisional holiness does not involve a crisis on our part. Hebrews 10:10— "By the which will we are sanctified through the offering of the body of Jesus Christ once for all." (The verb is in perfect tense.) In fact, sanctification or holiness comes into focus even in the first crisis work of grace. This is why we are beginning our study with birthing.

Concerning birthing as a heartbeat of holiness, let us then begin with considering that birthing is the Scriptural Beginning in Holiness.

1.1
The Scriptural Beginning in Holiness

ALL MY DAYS IN the holiness movement, I have heard of "two works of grace." Now, not as complex theology, but as convincing truth, I am personally and perfectly persuaded that the Scriptures set forth two crisis works of grace. I surely allow that some see holiness or sanctification only as a lifelong making of Christian improvement after being born again. From revelation and an openhearted searching of the Scriptures, however, I must also surely accept and steadfastly attest that for me the accurate truth is rather holiness is a momentary event— a crisis— as well as a maturing enterprise— a continuation; and that it is a making of holy changes only after the momentousness both of the first and of the second crises works of grace.

Note that the crisis of birthing is the scriptural beginning in holiness from the consideration of...

A. Intention

There are what we may call the "two wills" of scripture. 1 Thessalonians 4:3— "For this is the will of God, even your sanctification, that ye should abstain from fornication..." and 5:18— "In every thing give thanks: for this is the will of God in Christ Jesus concerning you." That will also includes verse 23— "And the very God of peace sanctify you wholly..."

The first text strikes me as not being the great proof text of entire sanctification that holiness preachers and teachers would make it. Observe that God's first will addresses fornication, which the Bible identifies as sin at its lowest point (1 Corinthians 6:16-20). Observe, too, that deliverance and abstinence from fornication has its source in sanctification (1 Corinthians 6:9-11). Observe, however, that God's second will of sanctification deals with the whole cleansed self— spirit, soul, and body. Observe, further, that the first is merely sanctification, while the second is a sanctifying, wholly or entirely.

It appears, therefore, that to be correct, we would do well to call regeneration (the new aliveness, or the first crisis work of grace) entrance sanctification; and reorientation (the new alignment, or the second crisis work of grace) entire sanctification. Both deal with sanctification, and the first is primary to the second. Intention, or the "two wills," has set the foundational principle that birthing is the scriptural beginning in holiness.

Note, also, that birthing is the scriptural beginning in holiness from the consideration of...

B. Intimacy

There are also what we may call the "two loves" of scripture. John 3:16— "For God so loved the world..." and Ephesians 5:25— "Christ also loved the church..." Observe that love, in the first place, is for the sinful world in order that it may receive life and not perish. This is entrance sanctification. The second love is for the spiritual wife in order that she may receive a loveliness, and be presented by Christ and to Christ. This is entire sanctification.

Note, as well, that birthing is the scriptural beginning in holiness from the consideration of...

C. Intercession

Similarly, there are the "two prayers" of scripture that relate to the two crises (1 Timothy 2:1-4 and John 17:9-11, 15-17, 20-21). Observe that the first prayer is for all persons, the bad and the blind, to be initially saved. This is entrance sanctification. The second prayer, however, is for special men, the believers and the blest, to be extensively sanctified. The believers were blessed, among other things, with life (verse 2); with a living likeness of God the Father (verse 6); with light (verses 8 and 14); and with loveliness (verse 22). They, however, needed to be specially sanctified (John 17:16-17, 19). This is entire sanctification.

Note, further, that birthing is the scriptural beginning in holiness from the consideration of...

D. Invitation

We come now to the "two special comes" of scripture. Matthew 11:28— "Come unto me, all ye that labour and are heavy laden, and I will give you rest. Take my yoke upon you…" And Matthew 16:24— "…If any man will come after me, let him deny himself, and take up his cross, and follow me." Observe that in the first passage, the commanding call is to come *to* Jesus for rest, and to take a yoke in companionship with Christ. This is entrance sanctification. In the second, however, the conditional call is to come *after* Jesus in renunciation, and to take a cross for crucifixion with Christ. This is entire sanctification.

As we continue this study of holiness heartbeats, we see more and more clearly that birthing is the scriptural beginning in holiness.

As a heartbeat of holiness, birthing itself is a Special Bestowal by Heaven.

1.2
A Special Bestowal by Heaven

BIRTHING, AS A BESTOWAL by heaven was first,

A. Symbolical

Bible readers know that the Old Testament bears much biblical symbolism. Old Testament physical types and pictures represent New Testament spiritual purposes and principles. There is, for example, the Tabernacle with its altars, its veil, its Mercy Seat, its Holy of Holies (Exodus 25-27). In the New Testament, the whole body of believers is the living temple of the Holy Spirit (1 Corinthians 3:16-17). The New Testament also refers to each Christian individually as the temple of the Holy Spirit (1 Corinthians 6:19).

Similarly, Paul uses Abraham's son Ishmael, by the servant girl, Hagar, in bondage, as a natural type of the Old Covenant. On the other hand, he uses Abraham's son Isaac, of Sarah, the free wife, as a spiritual type of the New Covenant. Galatians 4:22-23 — "For it is written, that Abraham had two sons, the one by a bondmaid, the other by a freewoman. But he who was of the bondwoman was born after the flesh; but he of the freewoman was by promise." Ishmael represents national belonging to God through the Law given by Moses, while Isaac represents new birth in God through life given by the Messiah.

The language of the context further highlights Isaac's being a type of birthing, or the new birth. Galatians 4:29— "...he that was born after the flesh persecuted him that was born after the Spirit..." The passage speaks of Ishmael as being born of the flesh, while it speaks of Isaac as being born of the Spirit. This language is symbolically identical to Jesus' great new birth statement (John 3:3, 6). In relation to the new birth, therefore, the symbolical Old Testament birth of the special son of Abraham, through Sarah, preceded and is a preview of the New Testament birth of the spiritual sons of the Almighty through the Spirit.

This symbolical representation of birthing reveals that birthing as a bestowal by heaven is...

B. Salvation

The account leading up to the birth of Isaac reveals that God brought Isaac to birth in spite of (1) Debate (Genesis 15:1-4 and 17:15-18); (2) Defilement (Genesis 16:1-4); (3) Derision and Doubt (Genesis 18:12); and Dishonesty (Genesis 18:13-15).

There is glorious gospel, not only in John 3:16, but also in Galatians 3:16 and Genesis 3:15. There is here the revelation that being in the line of the seed of Abraham, that led to Christ, Isaac is, by extension, not only symbolical of the new birth, but also of the new Bridegroom, Jesus, the saviour of the Church (Ephesians 5:23).

The moral deficiencies that are a part of the story of Isaac clearly show that birthing as a special bestowal from Heaven is a saving, not only from want, but also wickedness (Matthew 6:21) and weakness.

This symbolical representation of birthing reveals that birthing as a bestowal by heaven is also...

C. Supernatural

The supernatural is manifested in: (1) The Dysfunction of a Body (Romans 4:19a)— the undefined, temporary loss of virility (Genesis 16:15-16; Genesis 25:1-2); (2) The Deadness of a Birthing Chamber (Romans 4:19b)— the undeniable, tormenting lack of fertility. Genesis 11:30 is the first stark statement. Paul has his own striking presentation of this hopeless situation (Romans 4:18-20). God used the most extreme circumstances to show His mercy and His might.

The salvational and the supernatural say to us that any of us and all of us, whatever our prevailing condition, can experience birthing, for Abraham is father of us all (Romans 4:16). God, Who worked mightily for Abraham, is the same Almighty, Who through the mighty wind of His Spirit works supernaturally in our spiritual new birth (John 3:8).

Oswald Chambers says, "Our Lord's making of a disciple is supernatural. He does not build on any natural capacity at all" (*My Utmost for His Highest*). The outrageous, like Paul, can be courageous in coming for spiritual birthing (Acts 9:1-6). Outcasts, like the Syrophoenician woman, may be confident in claiming their spiritual birthing (Matthew 15:22-28). For whatever reasons, none need despair. Birthing is indeed a supernatural bestowal from heaven.

Birthing is more than symbolical; because it is salvational and supernatural, it is also...

D. Substantial

The new birth is no illusory emotional dream. It is no momentary mirage. It is absolutely factual life in Christ that is based on biblical verity and personal reality.

1. Teachings about this Substantiality

Immediately following the great call to holiness in 1 Peter 1:16, the Bible presents in several verses the reality of birthing. We may rearrange the presentation to offer a certain flow of operational order.

Concerning substantiality, there are,

a. *Foundational Facts* (verses 18-20). The born again have been told and have known the glorious gospel. It is the great good news that redemption is both priceless and timeless; and that even before the foundation of the world, God ordained His Son, Jesus Christ, to be the spotless Lamb Whose shed blood has bought royal redemption.

Concerning substantiality, there is,

b. *Fruitful Faith* (verse 21). Twice, in twenty-seven words, this verse locates the faith of the born again in God, Who raised His sacrificed Son from the dead and gave Him victorious, sharable glory. Faith is specifically not in some good feeling of being born again, but in God the Father Himself, Who is the Author of the new birth.

Concerning substantiality, there is also,

c. *Full Freedom* (verse 22a). The born again have been made free from sin. They have purified their souls in the sense that through the Spirit they have obeyed the truth of the gospel; but certainly their purity has come through the sanctifying Spirit (1 Corinthians 6:11).

Concerning substantiality there is, too,

d. *Faithful Functioning.* Faithful functioning consists, negatively, of (1) *That Which is Gone* (1 Peter 2:1). Gone is all Depravity— "malice"; that is, inherent or inborn evil that is a habit. Gone is all Deceit— "guile"; that is, adulteration of what is true, or other general fraud. Gone is all Dissimulation— "hypocrisies"; that is, pretending, like the falsely religious Pharisees, to being that which one is not. Gone is all Detractions— "envies"; that is, the feeling of pain or hatred over another's excellence or possession. Gone is all Defamation— "evil speaking"; that is, any slanderous talk against others, including backbiting.

Observe the note of repeated, sweeping totality expressed in "all." *All* evil functioning is gone, because in spiritual birthing God brings "out of darkness into his marvelous light" (1 Peter 2:9b).

There is, however, not only liberating loss. Positively and liberally, faithful functioning consists of (2) *That Which is Gained*. Gained is Desire— an intense longing and love for the Scriptures (1 Peter 2:2-3). Gained is Dependence— on "a living stone" (1 Peter 2:4), on "a chief corner stone" (1 Peter 2:6). This stone is no other than Jesus Christ the true foundation (Ephesians 3:20; 1 Corinthians 3:11). Gained also is Distinction— the spiritually born again become God's "chosen generation"— specially preferred; a "royal priesthood"— specially promoted; a "holy nation"— specially possessed; a "peculiar people"— specially purchased as His own (1 Peter 2:9). All of this distinction they never had before, but now they have (1 Peter 2:10).

Concerning substantiality there is, besides,

e. *A Fine Foreignness* (verse 17). Here on earth, the born again— like the great persons of faith of all ages— are only "strangers and pilgrims" (Hebrews 11:13; 1 Peter 2:11). They do not "pass the time" of their earthly "sojourning" in loving the world and the things of the world (1 John 2:15). In contrast, they busy themselves during their sojourning or "foreign residence" in loving, reverential deference to the eternal God, Whom they, as His children, call "Father."

In addition, concerning substantiality there is,

f. *Fulfilled Fellowship* (verse 22b). The born again not only have freedom from sin, they also have fellowship with the saints. They love fellow Christians with non-hypocritical, brotherly love (verse 22). This is the beauty of Christian discipleship (Romans 12:10). As tender affection exists between members of the same physical family, so members of the spiritual family manifest to each other the truest affection.

The beauty of brotherly love also includes fellow Christians "in honour preferring one another" (Romans 12:10b). Each longs, not to be honoured by the others, but each leads in esteeming the other as most valuable. The fellowship of the born again goes beyond. They also love fellow Christians with fervent, pure, divine love (verse 22). This is the badge of Christian discipleship (John 13:34-35). The heavenly Father loves unconditionally. In like manner those who are born again love without any consideration of the existence of grounds for love in others.

All of this — the facts, the faith, the freedom, the fulfillment, the foreignness, the fellowship — the 1 Peter passage, in summary, calls "being born again" (verse 23a). Further, this verb tense declares that their new birth is a present reality, in ongoing continuity.

Birthing is practical in its substantiality, and we note not only teachings about this substantiality, but also we joyfully note,

2. Testimonies to this Substantiality

My mother, born on the island of Saba— (God's Bible School is so wrapped up in my life) an evangelistic team from GBS went down the islands, went to this little island of Saba— never heard the gospel. My mother was an English catholic, an Anglican. She heard her first gospel message.

At the end of the message, the preacher said, "Is there anybody here who wants to accept Jesus Christ as Savior?" And my mother testifies that she jumped to her feet and said, "I do!" And in that very moment, God said to her, "You are born from above." Now you have to understand that the expression, "Born from above," is what we find in John 3:3, *you must be born again*. The meaning is, you must be born from above.

Here is Mother, not knowing the gospel, not knowing anything about the saving Word of God, and she gets a direct message from God: "You are born from above." Whoever said it, it must be true, that the altar is for slow seekers. The sunshine seekers just say, "Yes, God, here I am."

One lady was listening to an old minister of a holiness denomination years and years ago, talking about the Children of Israel going across Jordan, and he made the picture so clear, God was so present, that the lady said as she sat in her seat, *Why don't I just go across with them? While they're going, I'll go across with them*. And right there, in her seat, she went across the Jordan and into the Canaan land. We have a giving God.

Birthing or the new birth is not only symbolical and supernatural, the truth of God and the testimonies of these and other born again persons confirm that birthing is also solidly substantial.

Birthing, then, is not only the scriptural beginning in holiness and a supernatural bestowal by heaven, it is also about Spiritual Beloveds at Home.

1.3
Spiritual Beloveds at Home

BORN AGAIN PERSONS ARE God's beloved sons (and that includes daughters) of God (1 John 3:1a, 2a). Spiritual beloveds are first and foremost God's children at home. Home is one of the great emotive words, not only of social, but also of spiritual language and life. In his secular "Home, Sweet Home," John Howard Payne (1791-1852) spoke socially— possibly for all times— when he stated, "Be it ever so humble, there's no place like home."

Spiritually, home is incomparably dearer. The man in Luke's account of the Parable of the Lost— whether typified by sheep, coin or son— himself typifies Jesus, the Good Shepherd (John 10:11). The lost sheep, of course, represents "publicans and sinners" (Luke 15:1-4). All the sheep that Jesus finds He brings home (Luke 15:5, 6). Greater, therefore, is Will Thompson's "Softly and tenderly, Jesus is calling... Calling, O sinner, come home." Spiritual beloveds are beloved at home.

All beloveds are what I am calling...

A. Affection Sons

The expression "affection sons," like spiritual beloveds, means that spiritual birth sons and daughters are children whom the Father loves. How much does He love? This is expressed in John 3:16. Almost unspeakable, it is as great as His love for His Son (John 17:23).

This is declared by related words: "love" and "beloved" (verse 2). This love is not sexual love, nor merely social love, but spiritual love. English has only one word for love. In Greek this is not so. In John 21:15 the word is different than the word in verse 17. He used the same word Peter used.

Note first the,

1. Love for Affection Sons

1 John 3:1— "Behold, what manner of love the Father hath bestowed upon us, that we should be called the sons of God…" What love! The new birth is all about a God that loves us, the God Who wants to give us His life.

We have not only the statement in verse 1, but we have in verse 2, "Beloved, now are we the sons of God…" Affection sons. Again I go back, that we need to understand that God really does love us.

Our problem is that we have created our own gods. Self-divinity creates its own god and makes the god like itself. And because you are not able to express love as you ought to express love, you somehow think that God is not loving. But my friends, we have the wrong god. We don't have the right god until we understand that our God is a loving God.

God's special, saving love to us is *(a) Constant Love:* love not because we are loveable, but because God is steadfastly loving. It is *(b) Costly Love:* 1 Peter 1:18, 19— "Forasmuch as ye know that ye were not redeemed with corruptible things, as silver and gold, from your vain conversation received by tradition from your fathers; But with the precious blood of Christ, as of a lamb without blemish and without spot…" It cost God his all. God held back *nothing* of Himself in order to bring us back into His family and to bring us back home. "Precious," itself, does mean costly. However valuable the silver and gold may be, this value cannot be compared in any way to the costliness of the blood of Jesus Christ, the Lamb of God.

It is also *(c) Creative Love:* 1 Peter 1:23— "Being born again, not of corruptible seed, but of incorruptible, by the word of God, which liveth…" 2 Corinthians 5:17— "Therefore if any man be in Christ, he is a new creature…" God makes us new creations! New beings! When God comes into our heart he creates new life, makes us new creatures in Christ Jesus.

I don't know how God does it. None of us know the mysteries of created life. You see it in a little baby that mothers hold, and if you see it in little babies, certainly you see it in Christian babes that come into the Kingdom. God brings a new life into being.

Affection sons are real sons.

To further highlight "affection sons," note also the negative possibilities of,

2. Some Lacks in Affection Sons

Affection sons should not be Arduous Sons (Luke 15:29a). They should not be Abject Sons (Hebrews 12:5, 6). They should not be Apprehensive Sons— considering their heavenly Father as having a hard touch (Matthew 25:24-25) or a horrid taste (Luke 19:21). With God as loving Father anyone can change a bad, belittling earthly father image into the beautiful and blessed eternal Father image.

Some beloveds at home, however, are what I am calling…

B. Abortion-like Sons

We are purposely referring to this class of spiritual sons as "abortion-like sons." Physical abortion is so critical, so unnatural, and so unscriptural that without some clarifying comment the concept of spiritual abortion-like sons would be unavoidably repulsive. It is, of course, not our purpose here to discuss the utter wrongness of physical abortion. We may merely point out that the big question concerning physical abortion should not be whether one is pro-choice or pro-life. It rather is, solely, about being pro-creation and the Creator, and pro-life-giving and the Lord of Life— both inceptive of and of invested life (Genesis 1:20; 2:7; Job 33:4).

Briefly, we shall merely state some basic dissimilarities and similarities between physical and spiritual abortion. The term "abortion-like sons" is strictly spiritual and has reference to what may be a rare manner of coming to new birth in Christ. Spiritual abortion is unlike physical abortion in the fact that it is not the killing of God-created, God-supported, and God-delivered innocent fetuses (Psalm 139:13-16; 22:9). It is like physical abortion for the reason that the circumstances that precede some spiritual births being as symbolically traumatic as those are systematically traumatic that precipitate physical abortion, spiritual birth should not be possible. It is unlike physical abortion in the sense that spiritual abortion-like sons and daughters do, in spite of the circumstances, experience special miraculous mercy in being born again.

Note first,

1. Some Likeness of Abortion-like Sons

"Brother Saul" of Tarsus is God's most well-known abortion son. 1 Corinthians 15:8— "And last of all he was seen of me also, as of one born out of due time." Observe the marginal note at this place. The expression, "Born out of due season," comes from the rare use of the Greek word "born." It is not the same as the word for normal physical or spiritual birth (John 3:3, 4). It has reference to a wounded birth— a birth that is untimely or even unlikely. The main part of the combination word is the word from which we get our English word "trauma." Literally, it is an "out-of-trauma" birth, and is translated by the hopeless word "abortive." Paul had this kind of spiritual birth (Acts 22:4, 5; 26:9-11). Some, I now feel sure, have had a similar spiritual birth.

While I say I think that abortion sons are rare, I still feel abortion sons are real. One of the reasons why I say so is because I think I am an abortion son. Born in a Christian family, my mother and father ministers, my siblings coming to God early— my brother has never done anything else but preach the gospel, one of these boy preachers— but there was one in the family, and it was I.

I did not want the reproach of Christ. I did not want to go the gospel way. Somehow, those old saints turned me off. *Shouting saints, long-praying saints, long-sermon-preaching saints* (like I have come to be)... *Oh, if I could just go to that other church! Sermons short, nothing to put you under conviction. My friends are all there.* Oh, how I wanted to leave Father's home. But I was a prodigal that never got to the far country, because I kept running up against Jesus Christ.

I won't call myself the black sheep of the family. That is hardly a contemporary, acceptable word. It won't fit me anyway, because people who are "black sheeps" of my family could not be black. So it doesn't fit me.

But I was the prodigal son, who never got to the far country. I couldn't get there. I had gone into the church, because my father was now dead. My mother was concerned, I was beyond twenty, and she said, "Don't you think it's time for you to be in the church?" That was one of the good things God did for me, as naughty as I was, and as much as I didn't want the way, my mother's wish was my command. I made some adjustments in my life, and went down and argued with the preacher. Somehow, the arguments worked and I was baptized and taken into the church.

But while my church was in revival one night, I was out in a home with some friends. I did some playing on the piano by ear. I knew all the hit songs, and I was playing some jazz. My friends were dancing and while all this was going on I said, *But you have never danced. Why can't you find somebody to play and you do some dancing?* So I found somebody to play, and walked up to a young lady and said, "Will you dance with me?" And she said, "Who, *me?* With Reverend Taylor's son?" I mean, I can't even get to the far country!

Just about two weeks before that I was all set to go to the island of Curaçao and the oilfields, where every man had his own house, and I said, *This is what I've been living for.* But God put a heavy weight in my heart, and I asked them to scratch my name off the list.

Now, two weeks later, I am in this home and have this incident. I walked up to another girl: "Will you dance with me?" Of course she will. (There is always a daredevil around.) But my concern was that I have never danced. I don't want to step on the young lady's foot. So I'm rather nervous, and before I knew I ran right into a low ceiling lamp and broke the lamp. That was Wednesday. Come Friday, the man of the house comes in from his estate, and here I am, among my friends again. He simply said, "I notice my lamp is broken. I wonder how it got broken." That's all he said.

All of a sudden, a dagger went into my soul. I know what Paul must mean when he said, "It is hard for you to kick against the pricks." God put a dagger in my soul. I got sobered in a moment, not in church, not in a message— the Holy Spirit's taking a man's teasing words to convict me. Immediately I asked for an excuse and walked outside. I remember there was a storm coming in the east, and yet the west was still golden with the setting sun. Right there, I prayed. I said, "O God, my life is as angry as that stormy east. Please make it like the golden west." The rain began to come. I ran and sheltered, and ran and sheltered. I got to the service that night, and the preacher preached about that boy in the far country, who said, *Here I am, starving, and in my father's house, servants have enough, and to spare.* And he talked about enough joy and to spare, enough peace and to spare, enough forgiveness and to spare... I mean, he went on and on and on.

Then he said, "I have preached so long, I guess I better stop." There was a chorus of voices, "Go on!" He continued on, maybe an hour and a half that the gentleman preached that night, anointed, blessed. And then he said, "I have really preached so long, I will dismiss you people."

I remember my heart saying, *After you lay such a table? Dismiss?* I didn't wait to hear another word. I crumpled at the place of prayer, broken. I was as broken as anyone could be broken. But all the time I am praying and seeking God, somehow I am hearing, *But you will never be saved. You will never be saved.*

I rose from the altar, not satisfied. I walked home alone, no friends. I didn't want any snack that night. I got ready for bed, threw myself at my bedside, continued to seek God, and all the time I am seeking God, I think I am hearing, *But you will never be saved.* I am now exhausted physically and spiritually, and this is what I say to God: "God, I understand if you will never save me. I understand that, Lord. But Lord, I am serving notice right now that even if you never save me, I will never sin again." I fell into bed and fell asleep.

The next morning, I woke up born again. I used to

tease the theologians, "Explain how that could happen." Would you believe it was only about four years ago the Lord said, "Look, don't annoy the theologians any longer." (They don't know, anyway.) "I will tell you what happened."

And He said Father, Son and Holy Spirit saw me dying in spiritual childbirth, and decided to give me a C-section. And that's not Cæsarian; that's a "Christ section." The divine deliverer of babies knows how to bring you through.

"Brother Wingrove of the Caribbean." Only in the late 1900s did God reveal to me that this is what I should call my own spiritual birth.

Note also,

2. The Love for Abortion-like Sons

All that we have just said indicates that abortion sons tells of (a) Critical Love— Jude 22b: love that makes a difference. The Bible seems to point to this, also, as (b) Compassionate Love— Jude 22, 23: "And of some have compassion, making a difference: And others save with fear, pulling them out of the fire..." There are different interpretations of these verses. I must personally accept the emphasis that God knows how thoroughly to judge the situation of each seeking soul and He knows when emergency spiritual surgery is needed to bring a needy sinner to new birth. (c) Confirmed Love— Saul met God on the Damascus Road (Acts 9:1-6). He had gone back into Damascus, completely blind. He could not see. I do not know what kind of darkness he was going through. He keeps telling about what God did for him on the Damascus Road. He tells it three times. Here is Paul, in the darkness, and God sends a man by the name of Ananius, who comes to him and addresses him as "Brother Saul." That must have been one of the sweetest words Saul could have ever heard. *Who, I? A persecutor, now a brother?*

Shortly after my new birth I had an opportunity to come to God's Bible School. I remember coming into a camp meeting where people were shouting and praising God. Suddenly, I say, *I must not have anything. I am lonely, far away from home. Now I feel completely in darkness. Where am I? Who am I?* Those were the days when the school was going through some dark, deep waters.

There was a preacher, who came almost every year, by the name of Chief Charles R. Pamp-to-pee, a tall, towering, bronze-faced American Indian. He walked down from the platform. We were asked not to go to dinner that day. Some of us would have special prayer, choose prayer partners and find a place to pray for the school. While I was sitting there, in all of my bewilderment, I felt a hand on my shoulder. I looked up into the face of this towering preacher.

He said, "Taylor, you are my prayer partner."

I said, "Prayer partner? I don't even know if I am saved!"

He said, "That's why you are my prayer partner."

I tried to pray with the great preacher. Can you imagine? Just come to bible school, don't know where I am, feeling all the doubts and fears, and I have to pray with the evangelist. I prayed with him, and thank God for the encouragement. But then I leave school and I go off to New Jersey.

In a camp there, the first night I feel the fears. I say, *I have to hold onto my confidence.* And the second night, I am holding onto my confidence, but I have to confess, the grip is getting weaker. Tuesday night, it's weaker, and Wednesday night, it's weaker.

The last service I said, *Look here, Taylor. It doesn't make any sense to try to keep holding onto your confidence. Just let go.* I ended up at the altar, the only one there. They had a candlelight service planned for that night. Just one dear, old man prayed with me. I wasn't getting very far.

Finally, I went off to my cottage on the grounds, all alone. I prayed, 10:00 o'clock; 11:00 o'clock; 12:00 o'clock; 1:00 o'clock…

Somewhere around 2:00 o'clock, God came to a lonely Caribbean boy, and said, "What did I do for you on that rainy Friday night in February? What did I do for you?"

By now, I'm all broken, and I said, "You saved me."

And this is what God said: "Don't ever come back to Me again to ask Me if you're saved." Confirmed love!

Abortion sons are likely rare, but they are nonetheless real sons.

Like affection sons, all beloveds at home become…

C. Adoption Sons

Romans 8:15— "For ye have not received the spirit of bondage again to fear; but ye have received the Spirit of adoption, whereby we cry, Abba, Father."

Let us first look at,

1. Light on Adoption Sons

"Adoption" comes from a special word in Greek for "son" (*hyios*), except in Luke 2:48, where Mary refers to her new-found Son in the Temple as *teknon*. In many, many instances it has reference to the unique and special relationship that Jesus had with the Father as Son of God and Son of man (John 3:16-17). It is not the same as "sons of God" or "children of God" in reference to spiritual or born again sons (1 John 3:1, 2, 10).

This use of "son," here, refers to begetting or birth. Biblical adoption, on the other hand, seems not to be the same as social adoption. Socially, persons adopt children to bring into the family persons who are not theirs by birth. This type of adoption is absolutely wonderful, and no adopted child should succumb to inferiority.

Socially, however, a birth child is never spoken of as an

adopted child, nor an adopted child as a birth child. Spiritually, however, birth children are also adopted children (Romans 8:14-16).

All of this seems to suggest that spiritual adoption has an application different from social adoption. Socially, persons adopt children to bring into their family those who are not theirs by birth. Spiritually, God adopts us to bless in His family those who are already His by spiritual birth. It seems that we may see justification as addressing the legal implications related to our being sons of God: regeneration, the life implications; and adoption, implications of love and liberality.

Now let us consider,

2. The Love for Adoption Sons

Biblical and spiritual adoption suggests an application different from the social. I am coming more and more to sense that biblical adoption refers not to creative love but rather to (a) Closest Love— note "Abba," a term of intimacy used only in three references (Romans 8:15; Galatians 4:6; Mark 14:36). Biblical adoption does seem to refer to the closest love of special bonding rather than to the creative love of spiritual birth.

It refers also to (b) Crowning Love. Creative love gives one entrance into the spiritual family of God. The usages of "adoption" seem to proclaim, however, that this crowning love gives elevation in the spiritual family (Galatians 4:4-7). In this sense, the Christian's elevation from a mortal to an immortal body is also called an "adoption" (Romans 8:23).

It seems to follow, naturally, that this elevated status of adoption with its closest and crowning love relates also to (c) Consecrating Love (2 Corinthians 6: 14, 18). Note the expression, "sons and daughters" (verse 18). "Sons" is the word for adoption; and "daughters" has reference to being not only "a daughter of God," but also "acceptable to God, [and] rejoicing in God's peculiar care and protection."

We may say that, beyond Affection and real sons, and Abortion and rare sons, Adoption sons are royal and reigning sons, and that one of the ways they manifest this is through a radical relationship. It is clear that God expects of His "adoption" sons and daughters the special consecration of separation from all that is unlike Him, and of separateness for Himself alone.

Remember, therefore, that if in childhood we feel that we do not have very good human relations, in Christ we have not only heavenly relations of the perfect Father, but also the holy reality of priceless favour and preeminent fellowship and love of adopted sons.

Finally, birthing obviously must include Subsequent Bearing of Harvest.

1.4
Subsequent Bearing of Harvest

EARLIER WE SAW THAT birthing as a bestowal by heaven is not only symbolical and supernatural, but also substantial. It should not surprise, therefore, that birthing encompasses fruit bearing.

Six times in five verses, Matthew 7:16-20, Jesus associates fruit with corresponding character. Birthing and bearing go hand in hand. It is not great fervency that counts (Matthew 7:21). It is not great fame that counts (Matthew 7:22). What counts is good fruit (Matthew 7:20). Persons of the new birth manifest new behaviour. In a remarkable number of clear references, 1 John mentions fruit in direct relationship to birthing.

One fruit is...

A. Purity (1 John 2:29; 3:7-9)

Born again Christians are to be pure even as the heavenly Father is pure (1 John 3:3). Pure is, of course, one of the words that belongs to the holiness world family. Born again persons live pure lives. They manifest this by bringing forth the fruits of righteousness (1 John 2:29). Three times, in compact context, John emphasizes that the born again are unmistakably identified by their "doing righteousness" (1 John 2:29; 3:7, 10). They unvaryingly live righteous lives.

"In its broad sense, righteousness" (in the language of the Nelson Electronic Library) is "integrity, virtue, purity of life, rightness, correctness of thinking, feeling, and acting." In a narrower sense (as NEL continues) it is "justice or the virtue which gives each his due." Persons who are born again regularly bring forth good fruit, not the evil fruit of habitual sinning (1 John 3:9; 5:18a).

Another fruit is...

B. Charity (1 John 4:7-8).

Love here is divine love. It is the love that challenges us to love's excellent way even at the new birth (1 Corinthians 12:31-13:7).

A third fruit is...

C. Victory.

Birthing gives victory over (1) The World (1 John 5:4a). The born again overcome the world's *(a) Evil Actions* (1 John 2:15-16a); its *(b) Evil Attractions* (1 John 2:16b); and its *(c) Evil Ambitions* (1 John 2:16c).

Birthing also gives victory over (2) The Wicked One (1 John 5:18). We overcome the wicked one, because we are in Christ and Christ is in us, and because Christ overcame the Wicked One (John 14:30).

1.5
Conclusion

THE WONDERFUL REALITY of birthing is a heartbeat of holiness. It comes by Conviction (John 16:8a); by Conversion (Matthew 3:1-2); by Confession (1 John 1:9); by Contrition (2 Corinthians 7:10); and by Confiding (John 3:16).

2
BURYING
A Holiness Heartbeat

"Be ye holy; for I am holy."

"What shall we say then? Shall we continue in sin, that grace may abound? God forbid. How shall we, that are dead to sin, live any longer therein? Know ye not, that so many of us as were baptized into Jesus Christ were baptized into his death? Therefore we are buried with him by baptism into death: that like as Christ was raised up from the dead by the glory of the Father, even so we also should walk in newness of life. For if we have been planted together in the likeness of his death, we shall be also in the likeness of his resurrection: knowing this, that our old man is crucified with him, that the body of sin might be destroyed, that henceforth we should not serve sin. For he that is dead is freed from sin. Now if we be dead with Christ, we believe that we shall also live with him: knowing that Christ being raised from the dead dieth no more; death hath no more dominion over him. For in that he died, he died unto sin once: but in that he liveth, he liveth unto God." —*Romans 6:1-10*

Introduction

"HEARTBEAT" HAS REFERENCE to what is essential to life. In the light of the methodology of alliteration, I am of course using "burying," here, because it begins with the same alphabetical letter as birthing and belonging, etc. The reality behind the choice is that burying is similar in connection and outcome to crucifixion, and especially to death (Romans 6:3-8). The proposition, therefore, is that burying is essential to holiness.

In dealing with burying we are considering the old fashioned "death route." For some the death route has been a desperately difficult route. Some of us can understand why Ross Minkler, in his song, "Let Me Lose Myself," presented the agony of burying. There are many years of longing for rest and for perfect peace within the breast, and of seeking the Lord often, and "alone in tears." There is, however, a strange unwillingness to "pay the price" and "make the sacrifice." Therefore, there is wandering on and on for many years. In the chorus, there is "grief and pain" over losing self and finding it in the Lord, and over self being slain so that friends see only Christ. In another stanza, there is also the confession of how hard it was to die and "all self to crucify." I am convinced that there is a truer and better light in which to see and to settle burying.

The death route is indeed a dear route. We are not to "die like yellow dogs," but rather like yielded darlings. We shall see that burying is specially related to the core of intensive holiness; namely, that it is not enough to have a regenerating experience with the redeeming God, but that through burying there must be radical existence in the royal God. As birthing brings us into eternal life and love in the Redeemer, burying makes gloriously possible exclusive love and life with the Redeemer. Burying, then, is not heartache. It is a heartbeat of holiness.

Let us begin to explore the necessity and beauty of burying by first noting that the Scriptures Depict (or picture) Burying.

2.1
The Scriptures Depict Burying

BURYING IS PICTURED IN

A. A Typical Figure

We have been speaking of the "twos" of the crisis works of grace. We come to another. In terms of illustration, there are two gifts (Genesis 21:1-3 and 22:1, 2). In Genesis 21 we have a gift from God to Abraham of a son. In chapter 22, verses 1 and 2, we have a gift of Abraham to God. So God asks Abraham to follow the miraculous birthing or received gift of Isaac with the magnanimous burying or returned gift of his special son. One is a birthing, the other is a burying. It is so important a type that it is repeated in the New Testament. Hebrews 11:11— "Through faith also Sara herself received strength to conceive seed..." So that verse tells us about the birth of Isaac. In Hebrews 11:17 we have a separate paragraph, a separate act of faith: "By faith Abraham, when he was tried, offered up Isaac."

The Scriptures also depict burying in...

B. An Agricultural Figure

Again, we come to another set of "twos" that highlight the crisis works of grace. In terms of indispensability, there are two "verilys." John 3:3— "Verily, verily, I say unto thee, Except a man be born again..." — a birthing. Then we come to John 12:24— "Verily, verily, I say unto you, Except a corn of wheat fall into the ground and die..." — A birthing and a burying.

The "corn" or kernel of wheat that falls into the ground must naturally be a living seed. Farmers do not plant lifeless stones. The "verily, verily... except" of John 3:3 is therefore the logical and precious pair partner to the "verily, verily... except" of John 12:24. The first presents, in spiritual language, the miraculous producing or birthing of life. The second presents, in symbolical, agricultural language, the magnanimous planting or burying of the produced life. Both are crises, in Greek tense of action unrelated to time!

The Scriptures further depict burying in...

C. A Sacrificial Figure

I shall venture to say that once more we come to a set of "twos" that emphasize the crisis works of grace. In terms of imploring, there are two "beseechs." Romans 12:1— "I *beseech* you therefore, brethren, by the mercies of God, that ye present your bodies a living sacrifice..."

Look at 2 Corinthians 5:18-20— "And all things are of God, who hath reconciled us to himself by Jesus Christ, and hath given to us the ministry of reconciliation; to wit, that God was in Christ, reconciling the world unto himself, not imputing their trespasses unto them; and hath committed unto us the word of reconciliation. Now then we are ambassadors for Christ, as though God did *beseech* you by us: we pray you in

Christ's stead, be ye reconciled to God" (emphasis added).

"Beseech" is a calling that is intended to produce a particular effect. It comes from the root word, the Comforter. One "beseech" calls to reconciliation that relates to new birth (2 Corinthians 5:17). The other calls to a renunciation that results in a new belonging. Romans 12:1, itself, implies that Jesus' loving sacrifice, "the mercies of God," brought us to birthing or the beginning life of holiness. Now that same loving sacrifice leads us to burying as a living sacrifice, and this brings us to the abounding life of holiness.

These three figures— the typical, the agricultural and the sacrificial— proclaim the precious and profound principle that the supernaturally received life of birthing is to be followed by the sacrificially returned life of burying.

Very important to understanding the necessity of burying is the fact that Sin Demands Burying.

2.2
Sin Demands Burying

BURYING IS NECESSARY BECAUSE...

A. Sin Cannot Be Carried Away

We shall see that *sin* is not the same as *sins*. Sins or transgressions can be forgiven or sent away. Sin cannot be forgiven or sent away. 1 John 1:9— "If we confess our sins, he is faithful and just to forgive us our sins..." The meaning of "forgive" in this instance is that sins can be sent away. This general word, "forgive," means to send away.

2 Corinthians 5:21 says that He Who knew no sin became sin for us. Jesus, however, was both our sacrifice and our scapegoat— the strong goat of going away or departure or disappearing (Leviticus 16:5-10). He not only bore our sins, He bore them away (1 John 3:5).

Pilate, as false ruler, mockingly spoke, "Behold the man" (John 19:5b), and "Behold your King" (verse 14). But John, as forerunner, spoke meaningfully, John 1:29— "Behold the Lamb of God, which taketh away the sin of the world." What a carrying away this is! Psalm 103:10-12— "He hath not dealt with us after our sins; nor rewarded us according to our iniquities. For as the heaven is high above the earth, so great is his mercy toward them that fear him. As far as the east is from the west, so far hath he removed our transgressions from us."

Geographers tell us that this is a fitting expression to help us understand the completeness of the carrying away. There is a real point in not saying "as far as the north is from the south," because if you go so far north, you begin to go south, and if you go so far south, you begin to go north. But when you go east, you never go west, and when you go west, you never go east. You will never find your sins that God has taken away.

Unlike *sins* that can be carried away, *sin* cannot be carried away, because, whereas sins are deeds by which we disobey God in our living, sin is a disposition by which we dethrone God from our lives.

We may also consider that burying is necessary because...

B. Sin Cannot be Cancelled

Because sin is not the same as sins, sin cannot be cancelled, although sins can be.

Another meaning of "forgive" is to grant a favour, such as canceling our sinful debt. Luke 7:41, 42a— " There was a certain creditor which had two debtors: the one owed five hundred pence, and the other fifty. And when they had nothing to pay, he frankly forgave them both…" The creditor cancelled all debts, whether great or small. In the same way, the Creator forgives or cancels all sins, whether many or few (Luke 7:47a) and also cancels the sins of all sinners, whether they are chief sinners or only child sinners (1 Timothy 1:15; 2 Timothy 3:15).

Again, unlike *sins* that can be cancelled, *sin* cannot be cancelled, because *sins* refer to a debt that we owe, while *sin* relates to a depravity that we must own.

Sin can neither be carried away nor cancelled. What then is the answer? The answer is...

C. Sin Can and Must be Crucified

To come to grips with this need for crucifixion or burying, we must ask two supporting questions.
One is,

1. Why Must Sin be Crucified?

Either the word "sin" or "sins," or the way they are used in context, tells us that sin must be crucified, because while sins have to do with deeds that can be carried away or debts that can be cancelled, sin has to do with the disposition and depravity from which come the deeds and the debts (Ephesians 5:8; 1 John 1:10-17). In these verses, "sinned" (verse 10)— and therefore "sins" (verse 9)— refer to sinful deeds. In verses 8 and 7, "sin" is inherited sinful depravity or disposition. It is "a principle and power... exercising dominion over men" (Thayer). Elsewhere I read that it is "a determination of the nature of man as a personal power."

Sin must be crucified because this principle or power is,

a. A Devilish Divinity

It is devilish, because that is what Satan wanted — to dethrone God. And it is divinity, because Satan also wants us to dethrone God. Sin is the source of sins. Romans 5:12— "...by one man sin entered into the world..." That was the seed. When we trace it to its source, it takes us back to Genesis. (Genesis 2:7-9, 15-17; 3:1-5). We see that it is devilish divinity.

Spiros Zodhiates points out, in his *Hebrew Greek Key Study Bible* (p. 1617), that "'good and evil' (Genesis 2:9) is sometimes only an idiom of universality" (Numbers 24:13)— the domain of God, the unique One— "a compound unity made up of others" (Deuteronomy 6:4-5; Zechariah 14:9). Apart from this, the clear intention of the satanic serpent was to tempt man to be God (Genesis 3:1-5). When Satan came to Eve, he said,

"Ye shall not surely die: for God doth know that in the day ye eat thereof, then your eyes shall be opened, and ye shall be as gods…" Most of the Bible translations, including the NKJV, replace "gods" (verse 5) with "God." The temptation and man's tragic desire was to be like God. God, however, made man to be lower than God, not level with God (Psalm 8:4-9). Note that two trees were in the midst of the Garden (Genesis 2:9; 3:2, 3). The one obviously represented God's spiritual life that was shareable; the other, God's sovereign lordship that is singular.

What is carnality? Carnality is nothing more nor less than a devilish divinity, your wanting to be God, and my wanting to be God. That's it. Understanding that devilish self-divinity is the root sin, the carnal nature, that is to be crucified, makes clearer and surer the way to the victory of the beauty of holiness. When I am satisfied to be lower than God, that is when I am more nearly God-like. When I take my rightful place under God then is when real beauty begins to come out of my life, real Christ-like beauty. But any time I want to run my own life I can see and feel the ugliness and horror, almost in a moment. Go downstream from the source and the ending emphasis is that the basic, Adamic sin is devilish divinity.

Romans 6:6— "…knowing this, that our old man is crucified with him, that the body of sin might be destroyed…" When we come over to Romans 8:2 we hear about the law of sin. When we come over to 2 Thessalonians 2:3, 4 we read about the man of sin "who opposeth and exalteth himself above all that is called God, or that is worshipped; so that he as God sitteth in the temple of God, shewing himself that he is God."

The very nature of God makes room only for one God. The moment you have more than one god, you don't have any god, because God is supreme. God fills everywhere.

There can only be one God. So it is downright senselessness and sinfulness for us to want to be God.

We may say that sin must be crucified because it is,

b. Defective Divinity (Romans 7:18-24)

Adam grasped at being God, and his first act of divinity was making a leaf apron. Congratulations, Adam. What creativity. Before his fundamental and fatal folly, however, he had fluently given names to the entire animal kingdom. His second act was to hide from the very God Whom he sought to equal. And his third was the wonderfully manly act of blaming his wife. Wonderful, Adam. His acts of divinity were meager, miserable and mean.

Mastered by devilish and defective divinity, man today is just like fallen Adam. He is shut up to the meagerness of defective divinity. Today's humanity is mastering great modern technology (but it comes on the other side of the Cross) and it is not managing God's moral truth. Unspiritual human beings are miserable, hiding from God and from themselves, not among trees, but in work, sports, drugs, and even in religion. Man also is mean, but we shall come to this later.

Sin must also be crucified because it is,

c. Deceptive Divinity (Jeremiah 17:9a— "The heart is deceitful above all things...")

"Deceitful" is the word from which deceiving Jacob gets his name. It means *to seize the heel; to come from behind and throw down.* It refers to uneven land with deceptive drops that hinder upward ascent. The sin that is deceptive divinity makes foolishness seem to be wisdom. It makes wrong look like right (Isaiah 5:20-23). It conceals pride as humility.

In 1952, the summer after graduation, I needed to come back for a semester. Mother and I did some tours of camps and we got to the New York Binghamton camp. Rev.

Flexon was supposed to give the last message but he had an emergency and had to go away. The camp people came and asked me to preach. Here I am, just a greenhorn graduate from God's Bible School, and they've asked me to preach at this big camp.

I took it seriously. I went away and prayed, but when I came to the platform I would not sit on the front benches. So while I was sitting there on the second bench the Lord just simply whispered to me, "Don't you know that you can be just as proud on the second bench as on the front bench?" Some people act with such humility— *Oh, no, no. Not I. No, I don't want to do this.*— But down in their hearts they're saying, *I wish you'd give me a chance. Do it!*

Devilish divinity can deceive you. It can make pride look like humility. It can make anxiety look like concern, bossiness like helpfulness, stubbornness look like firmness, and anger look like righteous indignation. The greatest deception is that we do not recognize devilish divinity as our distinctive depravity.

Sin must therefore also be crucified because it is,

d. Depraved Divinity (Jeremiah 17:9b)

Sin makes us desperately wicked. It gives the nature of an incurable sickness beyond human power to change. It descends precipitously from Adam's despicably blaming his beloved to his son's deadly bloodying his brother. Depraved divinity is still the incurable spiritual illness responsible for the madness of sin-caused affliction, abortion and all abomination. It is also responsible for the meanness of self-caused animosity, anger and all aggravation— in ways such as being jealous, envious, anxious, suspicious, contentious, vexatious, factious, devious, duplicitous, ostentatious and even ferocious.

Sin that is devilish, defective, deceptive and depraved

divinity cannot be carried away, not cancelled, but thank God, it can be crucified.

We come then to the second question.

2. How is Sin Crucified?

The sin of devilish divinity is crucified by being,

a. Doomed in the Crucified Christ (John 17:19; Philippians 2:3-11)

Although God the Son created man, He humbled Himself and became man. "The incarnation was not a subtraction of deity, but an addition of humanity" (Believers Study Bible). As man, however, Jesus never grasped at being God.

In the wilderness temptation, the Devil wanted Jesus to make food to demonstrate Deity. But Jesus modeled faith by dedicating His humanity and delighting in Divinity (Matthew 4:4).

In the second temptation, the Devil wanted Jesus to manipulate fame to defend His Deity, but again Jesus modeled faith by depending on Divinity (Matthew 4:7).

In the third temptation, the Devil wanted Jesus to mimic the fall to dethrone Deity. But once more Jesus modeled faith by devotion only to Divinity (Matthew 4:10). He was not daring or distorting, but deferring.

When his mother said to turn water into wine, He said to her, "Woman, what have I to do with you?" After that He turned water into wine. I suggest that He went away and said, *Father, what am I to do? I don't take my orders from Mary. You tell me what am I to do.* And God said, *Go ahead and turn the water into wine.* So He came back and did because His Father said to. He depended on His Father. Having lived like that, He could then become our sin sacrifice.

From the beginning of His earthly existence Jesus never did His own will independent of the Father (John 5:19a;

6:38). To the very end of His days on earth, Jesus lived only to do the will of His Father (Luke 22:41, 42; 23:44-46). He lived virtuously. He died vicariously for man (2 Corinthians 5:21). He rose victoriously, having doomed sin forever (Hebrews 10:6-10).

The body of sin, with its devilish, defective, deceptive and depraved divinity, now therefore,

b. Sin Dies in the Crucified Christ (Romans 6:6)

When I graduated I chose as my motto Galatians 2:20, and I have had cause to rejoice that God has given me that as the golden text of my life: "I am crucified with Christ: nevertheless I live; yet not I, but Christ liveth in me…" By faith I know that terrible fellow, Wingrove Taylor, that selfish divinity, that he must die; that he does die; he has died, so that I can be free of all the horrors of being a self-made god. Now I belong to God, to live in God and with God.

We come to another of the "twos" of crisis grace. In terms of Injunction or Intervention there are two dealings with the old man (Ephesians 4:22-25; Romans 13:14; 6:6). Observe that in entrance sanctification we cast off the old man of sinful actions to be initially sanctified, but in entire sanctification we crucify the old man of self-almightiness to be intensely sanctified. Like the casting off, the crucifying is a crisis action. The death and resurrection of Jesus is so efficacious, it delivers decisively from the depraved sin-illness that eludes every attempted cure (conversion, control, correction) with the exception of crucifixion.

Burying, however, ought to be dying like a yielded darling, and not a yellow dog, when we understand that Spousal Life Defends Burying.

2.3
Spousal Life Defends Burying

SPOUSAL LIFE DEFENDS BURYING because burying is related to...

A. An Unchanged Spiritual Law (Romans 7:1-4)

This talks about the Law. This particular law has dominion over a man so long as he lives. God then uses an illustration. "For the woman which hath an husband is bound by the law to her husband so long as he liveth; but if the husband be dead, she is loosed from the law of her husband. So then if, while her husband liveth, she be married to another man, she shall be called an adulteress: but if her husband be dead, she is free from that law; so that she is no adulteress, though she be married to another man. Wherefore, my brethren, ye also are become dead to the law [not only to the Law, but dead to self, dead to everything, really] by the body of Christ; that ye should be married to another, even to him who is raised from the dead, that we should bring forth fruit unto God."

Here, the inspired Word completely ignores self-divinity's initiation or interpretation of marital dissolution to suit itself. Death as a removal from a former binding relationship to permit a future blessed relationship is not only a holy law but also the highest law (Matthew 19:3-6).

Now what God is saying is that He recognizes an unchanged spiritual law. One of the most thorny things in our world today is this whole business of marriage. There are hardly any homes, a small percentage of homes, that have not been touched by the massacre of marriage. Some people have not been able to see God's highest law in this area, and they've gotten remarried. There is not only a massacre of marriage, there is a marriage mess in this world.

I don't mean to hurt anybody at all. The point is, if I find myself in a marriage mess, I believe with all my heart that John 4 is my chapter— the lady at the well. When you get into all these marriage messes, only God can straighten us out. Unless God gives somebody a special directive, I am come to believe (I speak for my own self) that tearing up a house and moving away and all of that is not the best answer. What you need to do is to bring this whole mess to God. *I admit it. I acknowledge it. I thank You, that You are my source of living water.* I drink it, and I am humble, and I go out and testify.

She went out and spoke to the men. *Look, men. Come see a Man.* What she was saying is, *I have found the first and only Man there is in this world.* There is only one Man, the real Man, and I am only a man as I am a man in Christ Jesus. It is Jesus that teaches me to be a real man. And outside of that, these people that wear pants can be horrible people. She said to the men, *Look, I have found, for the first time,* THE *Man.* And then she knew how to be a woman to a man, by taking the wonderful Man, and became a flaming evangelist.

So no matter what happens to my life, I am not totally messed up, as long as I come to God. This word is not about tearing anybody and hurting anybody. Having said that, I believe that the Church of the Lord Jesus Christ ought to lift high the standard of God, the highest standard of God, that marriage is to be dissolved only by death.

If you cannot stand the abuse, if the man is beating you, bombarding you, tormenting you, my personal advice is, leave. If you can't stand the adultery and all of that, leave. But don't get married while he's alive. I believe God's highest standard is livable. They tell me about a lady who actually made up in her mind, *If you are going to sacrifice me, go on and sacrifice me, but I'm not leaving you.* And her loving sacrifice finally melted the man. I am not saying that your loving sacrifice will melt the man; you may be the sacrifice. He may actually kill you, though when he kills you, you go to heaven.

Life is serious business. If you can't stand the adultery, leave. I have made up my mind and I am not leaving. If my wife wants to play an adulterer, I am not even going to weep tears for all the other men she loves. I would not bless her with my tears. I will love her. I will support her. I will laugh with her, I will joke— but no bedroom privileges, for I cannot join my body to the body of a harlot. Don't tell me that I cannot live without sexual life. (The truth is, nobody is going to tell you, but one of these days, you are going to have to live without it. You will have passed your boundaries, passed your abilities, but you still have to live!)

Don't let the Devil fool you. He drives you, he torments you. That's because you live in self. But when you live in God, and God is your God, then you are big enough to do anything.

I am not talking about the normal "saved and sanctified" business, two trips to the altar. I am talking about the enormous God, the God of the universe, Who is able to do exceeding abundantly above all things. Somebody who doesn't happen to get married in life— do you know how many other things God can put into their lives to make their lives useful, meaningful? I am not trying to scare you. I hope you get married, if you can stand all the stress and make a go of it.

The unchanged spiritual law is that death must set you free. Even though the world is in a marriage mess, when it comes to the spiritual world, God will not change His law. The only way that God can enter into the entire sanctified relationship with us, is that we must experience what I call an unmerited spiritual liberty.

The outcome of burying is therefore related to...

B. An Unmerited Spiritual Liberty

I don't deserve to be free. I have this devilish self in me. But God has made a way through Christ, through His death, that I can put an end scripturally to my love relationship with my self. God sets us free when we die with Him.

The self dies. If the old man is now dead, the new man is now free. We have two men in us when we are born again. The old man and the new man, they live together for awhile. Even though God has given you new life, you still have the old man to contend with, and the old man is alive. But the moment your old man dies in Christ, you can say, "Lord, the deck is all clear. Everybody's gone. I am ready for You to come." And that's the only time He comes.

Isn't it wonderful that God gives us spiritual liberty? He is the Liberating Suitor. He liberates us from *(1) the Leading Suitor,* which is self (Matthew 16:24); and He liberates us from *(2) Lesser Suitors:* (a) The Statutes, the Law (Romans 7:4). You would be amazed how many of us are still tied up to Law, and we beat ourselves over the head about Law. The Law doesn't save us. It is the Lord Who saves us. (b) Society, Galatians 6:14— "But God forbid that I should glory, save in the cross of our Lord Jesus Christ, by whom the world is crucified unto me, and I unto the world." I am dead to the world. As I have indicated to people, I don't get my directions from Hollywood, but from Heaven; not from Paris, but from Paradise; not from New York, but from the New Jerusalem. (c) The Saints, Galatians 1:15-17— "when it pleased God, who separated me from my mother's womb, and called me by his grace, to reveal his Son in me, that I might preach him among the heathen; immediately I conferred not with flesh and blood: neither went I up to Jerusalem to them which were apostles before me…"

As you go on into chapter 2, beginning at verse 1, you will find that these dear saints in Jerusalem still had a lot to learn. They could only see God loving the Jews. They couldn't understand God's love for the Gentiles, so they lived a very narrow kind of life. If Paul had gone up to Jerusalem and those dear saints had gotten their hands on him, we might have never had an apostle to the Gentiles.

We are to respect all people— we are to respect our parents, our leaders, other Christians— but we must have a supreme respect only for God, because sometimes the saints can confuse you. You have to learn to stand up tall and be yourself in God. Listen into one ear, but think with your head. Listen, see what is worthwhile, but then you have to settle some issues with God. If I have to run to the scholars every time to say, "Can I say this?" I would have to walk around with a scholar.

I heard one man preach so close, and I am listening— and thank God, He has brought me to the place I can listen to truth without getting under dark conviction. My heart is open. If I have light to walk in, I walk in it. I feel freedom now while people are preaching, because that freedom has come in God. I remember when it was not always so— So he is preaching, and I am working through this thing, and suddenly it dawned on me, *Oh, I see, I see. Yes, I can live like he wants me to live, but I'd have to walk around with him in my pocket. And every time I'd say, Can I do this? How do I do that? Which way do we look? How do we stand?* Better still, I'd have to walk around with him on my back, a real burden. *What about it, brother?*

I am committed to God, and only God. I don't have all the answers, but I am willing to walk in the light. I don't have any resistance to the truth. I don't have any resistance about doing anything God wants me to do. Let Him speak to any other person, but I am going to weigh what I hear and see what God wants me to do.

You can get to the place where you are in bondage only to God, and when you are in bondage to God, you are free.

God knows some of us, that what we are doing is putting other people in bondage. I used to give light and try to walk in it for other people. Not any longer. It is not my responsibility to walk in light for you. Where would I get so many feet?

You give light, the other man must walk in it. Give the other man a chance to walk in it. Live your life before him. Let your light shine, but don't try to put the other man in bondage. I try to stay far away from everything that's called drugs, not only cocaine, but coffee. But I'm not going to be jumping down somebody's neck because they drink coffee. That's not what God wants me to do. There are some distinct things— adultery, lying, etc.— but there are some other areas, every man has to gain his own light. That is why we need, more and more, to teach truth from the Word of God so that people have light in which they can walk.

2.4 Conclusion

Now I know far more fully that burying for the sake of false self is vanity, agony and even impossibility, but burying for the sake of the freeing Saviour is victory, glory and blessed certainly (Matthew 16:25).

3
BELONGING
A Holiness Heartbeat

"Be ye holy; for I am holy."

"Wherefore gird up the loins of your mind, be sober, and hope to the end for the grace that is to be brought unto you at the revelation of Jesus Christ; as obedient children, not fashioning yourselves according to the former lusts in your ignorance: but as he which hath called you is holy, so be ye holy in all manner of conversation; because it is written, Be ye holy; for I am holy." —*1 Peter 1:13-16*

Introduction

WE ARE CONSIDERING heartbeats, or matters essential to the life of holiness. Each is absolutely essential to the one that succeeds. We have looked at Birthing as a heartbeat. We said that Birthing is about the Scriptural Beginning in Holiness; a Special Bestowal by Heaven; Spiritual Beloveds at Home; and Subsequent Bearing of Harvest.

We next dealt with Burying. We must pause to emphasize that without birthing, we have nothing worth burying (John 12:24). If I don't have a living seed I can't plant a seed. Concerning burying, however, the Scriptures Depict it, Sin Demands it, and Spousal Life Defends it.

We come now to Belonging as an essential to holiness. Again we emphasize that without burying there can be no belonging. Burying makes possible belonging. We may belong lovingly and entirely to God only after burying. That alone gives the right to belong legally and exclusively to God (Romans 7:1-4).

We might call belonging the central pulse of the heartbeats. Birthing and burying are requirements for belonging, and what follows— blessing and becoming— are results of belonging. Let us look at the Basis of Belonging.

3.1
The Basis of Belonging

BELONGING IS BASED ON what we may call—

A. Definition (or Meaning)

The concept of belonging comes from the word, "holiness," itself. By extension, it comes from the extensive "holiness" word family. Throughout the Old Testament and the New Testament this word family includes words such as chaste, clear, consecrate, dedicate(ed), hallow(ed), holiest, holiness, holy, pure(ness), purification, purify (with its tenses), purity, saint(s), sanctification, sanctify (with its tenses), and sanctuary. This word family carries two distinctive meanings.

One meaning clearly is.

1. Saintliness before God

God requires saintliness in the Old Testament. Leviticus 11-15 and 18-23 are full of this application of saintly behaviour. In these chapters, there are carefully constructed categories of behaviourial constraints that are punctuated by a recurring chorus of holiness. There is the full chorus, Leviticus 11:44, 45— "For I am the LORD your God: ye shall therefore sanctify yourselves, and ye shall be holy; for I am holy: neither shall ye defile yourselves with any manner of creeping thing that creepeth upon the earth. For I am the LORD that bringeth you up out of the land of Egypt, to be your God: ye shall therefore be holy, for I am holy."

That's a full chorus. As you go through the Book of Leviticus, you will find a medium-length chorus (20:7, 8); a short chorus (19:2); a shorter chorus, 19:3b— "I am the LORD your God"; and even the shortest, 19:12— "I am the LORD."

These constraints cover a variety of subjects: Sanitary behaviour (chapters 11-15); Sacrificial behaviour (Leviticus 16:2-17:15); Sexual behaviour (Leviticus 18:6-20, 22, 23; 20:10-21); Spiritual behaviour (Leviticus 19:3-8; 20:1-6); Social behaviour (Leviticus 19:9-18); and Sacerdotal behaviour (Leviticus 21:1-21, 23-22:9). The entire spirit of the New Testament makes the same requirement of saintliness (Ephesians 4:17).

Here is this marvelous relationship of God. Because of Who God is, it determines who I must be. One man tells me that, as his son would leave home, or his daughter, they would have a little parting expression: "Remember whose son you are." "Remember whose daughter you are." So I must behave because I have to remember Whose son I am. I am God's son, and because God has a certain standard of living then I, too, must be blessed with a certain standard of living.

Noticeably in the Leviticus passages with its recurring choruses, but also in the Ephesians passage, the holy God, the Person, is at the center of these behavioural constraints (Ephesians 4:18, 20, 24, 30). A Caribbean youth rightly noted that the Church gives precepts, but few principles. We may point out that both precepts and principles are always to be related to the divine Person. Less, even, do we relate the conduct of our holiness to companionship with the holy God. This is so because we too little taught the other meaning of the holiness word family.

The second meaning is,

2. Set Apartness unto God

The concept of set apartness is as prominent as saintliness. Leviticus 20:26— "And ye shall be holy unto me: for I the Lord am holy, and have severed you from other people, that ye should be mine." Always, the sanctified God must be able to say of the sanctified, "They are mine." Set apartness is as potent and as present as saintliness. Both concepts are sometimes given side by side (Deuteronomy 7:6-8a, 9, 11).

One doctrinal position stresses the set apartness aspect of holiness. The position we hold stresses the saintliness aspect. Maybe it is altogether my fault, but in all the years of my up-growing in the midst of our doctrinal emphasis, I have known only the saintliness aspect.

One of the tragedies of the holiness movement is that we have emphasized the behaviour, but we have not emphasized the belonging. We are so on edge about being holy that we can't be happy.

Now I understand that, apart from behaving, God wants me to belong to Him. Out of belonging, really comes behaving. The opposite position may have the language of set apartness without the highest behaving, but then we have the life of saintliness without the heartiest belonging. I will not speak for other positions, only our own.

Why do we put asunder what God hath joined together? 1 Peter 2:9— "But ye are a chosen generation, a royal priesthood, an holy nation, a peculiar people…" Note: "peculiar," as you know, does not mean we are odd people, but God's people. The word means "one's own" or "special." The sanctified are God's own, special people.

"...That ye should shew forth the praises of him who hath called you out of darkness into his marvellous light." Isn't it a marvelous thing, to have an opportunity to walk around the world manifesting the excellences of God. A powerful meaning of sanctification or holiness is belonging to God and God alone. We sing, "Jesus is all I need." In fact, Jesus *is* all we need, because Jesus is all we have.

We do not need to fear (often an unrecognized carnal or idolatrous trait) that the companionship represented by set apartness will weaken the conduct of saintliness. Actually, true set apartness only enhances saintliness.

For example, set apartness will deal decisively with selective righteousness. Pharisaic-like, it is possible to not gamble but gossip; to not curse but covet; to not drink alcohol but display annoyance; to be plain in attire but prejudiced in associations; to be circumscribed in holy deeds but compromising in worldly display. Set apartness will change all such selective righteousness into sweeping righteousness.

Without absolute set apartness, we will possess our friends, ministry, burdens, possessions, etc., and when we do so, we pollute them, for God is the true, the only Possessor (Mark 10:17-22; Luke 12:16-20). On the other hand, whom and what God possesses He purifies (Hebrews 12:6-10).

When He possesses us and the persons greeting, loving, blessing, honouring us, we will see such persons as doing all these to Him. When, therefore, they also do all these things to others, we will not be jealous, because these they also do to Him (Matthew 25:34-45).

The summary is that set-apartness or radical belonging, and the cleansing that accompanies it, produces royal behaving as nothing else can.

We may add that belonging is also based on what we may call...

B. Designation (or Naming)

In the KJV, of some fifty words that appear as "belong," "belonged," "belongest," "belongeth," or "belonging," only four have a direct word relationship. In none of the four does the word carry the direct meaning of "belong."

In translating the scriptures the translators have given what I call,

1. Grammatical Designation

In the three New Testament places, each word translated as "belong" is actually the verb, "to be" (Mark 9:41; Luke 23:7; Hebrews 5:14). Only the first is relevant to our subject. Mark 9:41— "For whosoever shall give you a cup of water to drink in my name, because ye belong to Christ, verily I say unto you, he shall not lose his reward."

Here, the word conveys that the disciples are Christ's, or exist for Christ. This, to me, is more than wonderful. God and God alone is the self-existent I AM (Exodus 3:14). We may say that the disciples *are* only because God *is*. Similarly, everyone and everything that is or exists, is or exists because God is the only eternal, existing One (John 8:58). It follows, therefore, that everyone and everything belongs to Him (Luke 2:22, 23). It follows that to be is therefore to belong to God.

In the one Old Testament reference that has a direct word relationship, "belong" carries only,

2. Compositional Designation

We have one other "belong" that has a word meaning. It is in Esther 2:9— "And [Esther] the maiden pleased him, and she obtained kindness of him; and he speedily gave her her things for purification, with such things as belonged to her…"

"Such things as belonged" to Esther, actually means

the things appointed or assigned to her. All the things that Esther got belonged to the king. They were hers in name only.

Isn't it marvelous to know that whatever things we have, have been appointed to us by God? I am not going to be jealous of anybody. Let God appoint to anyone what He will, because the same God who appoints to you is the same God who appoints to me. Everything belongs to God. I can't tell God that He should not appoint more to you than He appoints to me. It is all His. You are His; I am His. All the appointments are His, and I am just very grateful and thankful to God for what He gives me.

So I can walk through life not envying anybody. I can walk through life not pitying myself. Whatever I have I don't deserve, anyway, and God has been so good to give me some appointments. All is God's. All we have is only assigned to us. Persons, things and immaterial possessions that we may have are all God's. They belong to us in name only.

So the word "belong" there means appointment.

We come to the beauty of the thing, because there are only four of these "belong" words that have any connection to word relationships. The others do not even exist. In forty-six references, my understanding is that a verbal word is absent altogether, and the KJV "belong" or other of its forms is only supplied to make sense in translating the original to English.

In Genesis 40, Joseph is in prison and some of his fellow prisoners have a dream. In verse 7 Joseph sees that they look so sad and he wants to know why. Verse 8— "…they said unto him, We have dreamed a dream, and there is no interpreter of it. And Joseph said unto them, Do not interpretations *belong* to God?"

Notice in your Bible the word "belong" is in italics. The word is not even there. The word has been compositionally designated to make English sense to us. So literal readings seem to be, for example, "Interpretations... God" (Genesis 40:8); "secret *things*... the Lord" (Deuteronomy 29:29); "To me... vengeance, and recompense" (Deuteronomy 32:35); "Salvation... the Lord" (Psalm 3:8a); "the shields of the earth... God" (Psalm 47:9b); "O Lord, righteousness... thee" (Daniel 9:7a).

What this is telling us is that every person, object, ability and emotion— after all there is in the entire vast and mysterious universe— we must place the cardinal and solitary word "God." Everyone and everything, God's! I don't want to be a highway robber, to be stealing from God. If it is His, I am going to leave it His. If I am God's I am going to leave myself God's.

Isn't it wonderful to know that whenever you are in a difficult situation and you are searching for interpretations, you don't have to get all torn up in mind. Just hold steady, for interpretations belong to God. Somebody illtreats you, don't get all worked up. Vengeance and recompense belong to God. War rages everywhere, we don't need to get disturbed. The shields of the earth belong to God. Our God is the big, wonderful God Who possesses everything we can possibly need. We don't have all the answers, but we can rest in Him until He comes through with answers.

Everything being and belonging to God are supremely inseparable.

We may add that belonging is also based on what we are calling...

C. Design (or Making)

Precious prepositions (relational words) proclaim that we are made to belong to God only. 1 Corinthians 8:6— "...but to us there is but one God, the Father, of whom are all things, and we in him; and one Lord Jesus Christ, by whom are all things, and we by him." Everything comes from God. See that little preposition, "of." All things come from Him, and we are in Him.

Colossians 1:16, 17— "...for by him were all things created, that are in heaven, and that are in earth, visible and invisible, whether they be thrones, or dominions, or principalities, or powers: all things were created by him, and for him: and he is before all things, and by him all things consist" or hold together. Whenever I feel a temptation or pressure to go to pieces, I just go further into God, and I can't go to pieces. The pressure is on to make me addled or upset or whatever it is, and I just hide more and more in God. I find myself not going to pieces.

We are formed by Him, to fellowship with Him and function in Him. Then we will be fruitful through Him, always flowing towards Him, and finishing in Him. Formed by God, and functioning through Him, we are to finish at Him, our goal, our God.

Romans 11:36— "For of him, and through him, and to him, are all things: to whom be glory for ever. Amen." Who gets the glory? God. Why does God get the glory? Because only He deserves the glory. I don't have to worry about getting any glory. I don't deserve any, anyway. But while I'm with the God Who gets the glory, some little bit of glory becomes mine, and yours.

All who live any other way are broken-off, barren branches fit only to be burned (John 15:5, 6). All who live any other way are not only sorry sinners but the foremost fools (Luke 12:16-21).

Belonging is indeed the central heartbeat of holiness.

We have looked at the Basis of Belonging. Definition, Designation and Design unquestionably establish it. We truly belong to God.

We need now to inquire into the nature of this belonging. We therefore must consider the Boundaries of Belonging.

3.2
The Boundaries of Belonging

BELONGING CALLS FOR BOUNDARIES that are...

A. Extensive

Boundaries are extensive in,

1. Domain

1 Thessalonians 5:23— "And the very God of peace sanctify you wholly; and I pray God your whole spirit and soul and body be preserved blameless…"

Theologians differ as to whether man is a threefold or a twofold being. The KJV Study Bible suggests, "This verse does not form a definition of the constituent parts of man, but is a Hebraism to denote the whole man." We shall not burden our minds here with these differences. We shall simply say that this scripture before us indicates that belonging applies to the sphere of man's being that we shall call—

a. General Domain

Belonging takes in the spirit (our upward and spiritual capacities). Our spirits belong to God (Ecclesiastes 12:7).

In the domain of soul and its interrelationships with persons and things, we are also to belong to God. Whatever the domain under consideration, we are to belong solely to God in that area of activity or capability. I must not try any kind of relationship with anybody except as I have that in God. It is not what I like, not what amuses me, not what excites me, but all of my relationships must be in God, because my soul belongs to God. We are not to gratify ourselves but to glorify God alone (1 Corinthians 6:19, 20).

Belonging includes not only our spirits and our souls but extends, then, to take in the body (our earthward and physical capacities). Our bodies belong to God (1 Corinthians 6:19).

The scriptures declare that we are to belong to God also in what we shall call,

b. Supplemental Domain (Deuteronomy 6:4, 5)

The Bible expresses extensiveness in supplemental domain by using the love language of belonging. Note the fullest account, Mark 12:29, 30— "The first of all the commandments is, Hear, O Israel; The Lord our God is one Lord: and thou shalt love the Lord thy God with all thy heart, and with all thy soul, and with all thy mind, and with all thy strength..."

We are to love the One to Whom alone we directly belong with the "heart" (i.e., fundamentally, in the center of the divine and devotion); with the "soul" (i.e., freshly, in the center of drives and desires); with the "mind" and "understanding," verse 33 (i.e., finesightedly and farsightedly, thinking, in the center of discernment and discrimination); and with the "strength" (i.e., forcefully, in the center of dynamism and doing).

John Wesley's comment on verse 33 is that human beings are to love and serve the Lord "with all the united powers of the soul in their utmost vigour." Listless loving and saltless serving are not ways of holiness.

Belonging is to be extensive not only in domain; Deuteronomy and other Books of the Bible add extensiveness in,

2. Deeds

Belonging includes not only extensive loving of the Lord God (Deuteronomy 6:5; Mark 12:30); but also extensive seeking (Deuteronomy 4:29), serving (Deuteronomy 10:12), obeying (Deuteronomy 26:16; 30:2), cleaving unto (Joshua 22:5), walking before (1 Kings 2:4), and walking after/keep commandments (2 Kings 23:3), turning to (2 Kings 23:25). The New Testament adds the sweeping "whether" and "whatsoever" of deed (1 Corinthians 10:31); and then adds to these the "whatsoever" of declaration (Colossians 3:17). This includes doing or saying, "in the name of the Lord"; that is, by Jesus' prerogative or right in His power, for His praise, and after His pattern.

The boundaries of belonging are not however only extensive in domain and in deeds, they are also...

B. Exhaustive

We are to belong to God and God alone not only totally but also wholly.

Belonging is therefore exhaustive in,

1. Dimensions

In reference to sanctification of spirit, soul and body, note the qualifying word, "whole" (1 Thessalonians 5:23). Then in reference to loving God with heart, soul, mind, strength and understanding, note the qualifying word, "all" (Mark 12:30, 33). "Whole" is a combination of two words, but its dominant, controlling word is the same as "all." It is interesting that "whole" qualifies by position (at the beginning) while "all" qualifies by repetition. Both words, along with the methods of qualification, emphasize the totality of whatever is so qualified. These qualifying concepts and characteristics declare that spirit, soul and body; and heart, soul, mind, strength and understanding belong exhaustively, and therefore exclusively, to God in all dimensions, in all parts, with no part lacking. We are to belong to God not only in all of the domains of our being, but also in all the dimensions of those domains.

There is more to exhaustiveness than the dimensions of it. We are to belong to God exhaustively also in,

2. Degree

In 1 Thessalonians 5:23 there is not only the adjective "whole", but also there is the adverb "wholly." In the Greek it is the verbal adjective form of "all," and means completely and entirely. The emphasis of wholly or entirely appears to be not on the sanctifying action of the God of Peace, but on us, the sanctified agents. He sanctifies, wholly and entirely, us. The German word for "wholly" translates as "through and through." The literal translation from the French is the double-edged, "all entire"; that means completely.

We are to belong to God not only in all of our domains of being and in all the dimensions of all of our domains, but also the deepest depth and farthest distance of every part and dimension. Our being sanctified is far more exhaustive than we can ever comprehend. Radical set apartness to God involves radical saturation by God.

Furthermore, to all of this exhaustiveness in dimensions and degree, "wholly" adds the thought of exhaustiveness in,

3. Duration

"Wholly" not only carries the meaning of entirely — to the full end — but also of eternally — to final endlessness. We are to belong to God not only exhaustively in all the dimensions of our being, and in all of the degrees of those dimensions, but also we are to belong thus to God interminably. In the darling doctrine of holiness, we say to God, "Forsaking all others, we keep ourselves only to You so long as..." In the words of the song, "Now I Belong to Jesus," this means, "Not for the years of time alone, but for eternity." A Canadian Christian lady, electric and alert in her eighties, testified that her love for God and her belonging to God is unrivalled and irreversible! — and we might add, interminable.

The boundaries of belonging are indeed not only extensive and exhaustive, but also...

C. Exclusive

By instruction, by inference, or by implication, it is clear that in principle and in essence we are to have an exclusive relationship with God. We are to worship and serve him only (Matthew 4:10). Inferentially, it is He alone that we are to love (Mark 12:30). Set apartness is so entire that uniquely we belong to God alone (1Thessalonians 5:23).

We may note that,

1. Doctrine Declares this Exclusiveness (1 Corinthians 6:20a)

"Bought with a price" is not a cost that represents our intrinsic value or anyone else's interested value, but God's own redeeming invested value. The value of the holy is truly incalculable. Bought by Christ and made so supremely valuable, the holy belong to God and no one else. Purchase requires that we belong only to God Who bought us.

We may note also that,

2. Dwelling Demands this Exclusiveness (1 Corinthians 6:19)

More truly than God dwelt in the Old Testament places of worship, He completely dwells in persons made in His image and after His likeness. "Temple" suggests the entire area of the sanctuary. As His temples we are set apart for God's service alone; that is, exclusively. He fills all creation and especially does He fill the Church, the Body of Christ (Ephesians 1:23). Possession requires that we belong to God alone Who fills us.

Further, we may note that,

3. Dear Demand Defines this Exclusiveness (1 Corinthians 7:23)

"Be" is an imperative, or word of command. "Not" is the conditional subjective negative. We might call it the appealing or agreeable negative. It is God's prerogative to make absolute demand of His lordship over us on the ground of redemptive purchase. In graciousness, instead, He makes it affectionate demand. We have here a profound teaching. A holy person may actually be a slave, socially. Still such a person is, in a marvelously lordly way, to be "the Lord's freeman" (1Corinthians 7:22a). Similarly, a holy person may be a freeman, socially. Still, such a person is, in a magnanimously loving way, to be the Lord's bondservant.

We have here a profound truth. Wholly dedicated to God, our heavenly relationship with God is utterly total. Therefore, whatever our human relationships, those relationships are uniquely tributary. Supremely, we belong to God alone. In all of our earthly relationships, we are to act, in the language of the Family Bible Notes, "from supreme regard" to God alone. This sovereign relationship takes precedence over all others, and determines the nature of our relationship with any others. Principle requires that we exclusively belong to God, Who alone is our loving Master.

God's purpose surely is that we take this exhaustiveness of belonging seriously and practically. We therefore are to love and belong directly not to ourselves, not to our closest relatives, and not to any others. We are to belong to God and God alone. In the Vine, no branch belongs to another branch. Each rather belongs to the Vine (John 15:2).

If I belong primarily to God, then I can belong secondarily to myself or others, and the secondary can rival the primary. When I belong solely to God, there is no rivalry. Then I am free to comply with God's glorious right that I belong to Him and Him alone, and also to carry out my God-given responsibility to be to others, and to myself, what God wants me to be!

Belonging is a scriptural concept, and a sweeping condition. All this must not overwhelm us. Belonging is indeed the sublimest choice.

We close this study, then, by looking at the Blessedness of Belonging.

3.3
The Blessedness of Belonging

THE SONG OF SOLOMON IS ALSO called the Song of Songs. This in Hebrew idiom means "the most excellent of all songs," or we might say the mother of all songs. There are divergent views concerning this Book. This is not the place to enter into the arguments. The Song of Solomon is a part of the Scriptures. Some, like John Wesley, in the light of Psalm 45, consider it an elaborate allegory of Christ and the Church. Jamieson, Fausset, and Brown liken it to "A foretaste on earth of the 'new song' to be sung in glory (Rev. 5:9; 14:3; 15:2-4)." We cannot deny that it speaks with engaging language about the love of choice relationship. From it, we borrow some vital views on the bounty of belonging.

There is in it, first, the blessedness of...

A. Decisiveness

Song 7:10a— "I *am* my beloved's..." You see the *am* is supplied again: "I... my beloved's. In relation to belonging, the passage is one of the examples where interpreters have supplied verb forms to complete the English sense. The NAB is among versions of the Bible that directly state, "I belong to my lover." Using the verb, "to be," and thus linking being to belonging, the KJV rendering is, "I *am* my beloved's."

This completed statement, "I am my beloved's," rings with a freedom from doubt or wavering. It is a wonderful thing, to have this sense of decisiveness. There is no hope-so hesitancy in this language of love, only clear-cut certainty that flows from rugged reality.

What a marvelous thing it is to be able to say, I *am* God's; not, I feel God's; not, God has blessed me, therefore I am God's. But I have made a commitment by the power of Jesus Christ, and I *am* my Beloved's. Isn't it nice to get beyond the doubts? Settle it.

There should be nothing surprising about this. Because we know the facts of our relationship with others, there is no doubt or wavering that we belong to earthly others — wife, children, friends, church, etc. For example, a husband knows he belongs to his wife. He knows that he agreed to marry her and that she agreed to marry him. He knows, along with the lady who is now his wife, that he went to the marriage altar. He knows he said Yes to the various vows. He knows that, along with his bride and witnesses, he signed the marriage record. He knows beyond doubt that he belongs to his wife.

Even more real in the spiritual realm, God knows and we know that we have been "born from above" (Romans 8:16). God knows and we know that we have denied ourselves and have taken up the cross to follow Jesus. God knows and we know that, having decisively lost our life for His sake, we find it (Luke 9:23, 24). God knows and we know that we have died to all other suitors and have become His and His alone (Romans 7:4).

Far more surely, therefore, are we absolutely assured that we belong to the eternal Other. From time to time, I turn my heart to God and affectionately say, "Do You know that I am Yours alone?"

Immediately there is the divine response (indeed a witness of the Spirit) saying, "I know." Belonging is the glorious guarantee of decisiveness, the great dissolver of doubt!

This book of belonging also speaks of the blessedness of...

B. Distinction

The blessedness of distinction comes through association of belonging to the One of supreme importance. Because the glorious girl in the Song of Song belonged to the King of Kings, she manifested a deep, daring, and demanding devotion (Song 5:8). When others heard her strong sighing and lamentable longing for her beloved, they asked the lady lover a question almost stinging with sarcasm: "What is thy beloved more than another beloved...?" (Song 5:9a) In response to her critics, she lauded her Lover with a liquid litany of His loveliness that made her lordly. She understood that in Him resided the epitome of excellences. C.I. Scofield put it this way: "There is in Jesus a perfect equipoise of various perfections. All the elements of perfect character are in perfect balance. His gentleness is never weak. His courage is never brutal."

The lady lover spoke her own strong sentiments. She declared that He is the finest (Song 5:10a— His complexion is the most pleasing mixture of "white and ruddy"). He is the chiefest (Song 5:10b— He is above all others as standard bearer). He is the purest (Song 5:11a— Like "fine gold," He is pure as that originally mined). He is the highest (Song 5:11a— He is the head of gold. Compared with Him, others are brass, iron and clay). He is the youngest (Song 5:11b— His "locks are bushy and black." Eternity cannot age Him). He is the keenest (Song 5:12— Nothing escapes His clear, calm sight, but His seeing is also compassionate). He is the sweetest (Song 5:13, 16a— His face, features and the form of His lips and mouth are full of fragrance). He is the stateliest (Song 5:14— No jewel or combination of them excels His royal form). He is the strongest (Song 5:15a— No columns of "marble set upon sockets of fine gold" are stronger than his strength and steadfastness). He is the comeliest (Song 5:15b— The cedars of Lebanon only illustrate His beauty). He is the most desirable (Song 5:16— Language breaks down, and she can only blushingly proclaim His absolute loveliness).

Far more contemporary lovers pick up the sweet song. An anonymous lyricist has penned:

Fair are the meadows;
Fairer still the woodlands,
  Robed in the blooming garb of spring.
Jesus is fairer,
Jesus is purer,
  Who makes the woeful heart to sing!

Fair is the sunshine,
Fairer still the moonlight,
  And all the twinkling, starry host.
Jesus shines brighter,
Jesus shines purer,
  Than all the angels heaven can boast!

We know who we are— the poorest and the feeblest. We know Who He is— the purest and the finest. In fact, we know that the Lord, our Lover, is really incomparable (Isaiah 40:18; 46:5). As Scofield said, "All other greatness has been marred by littleness, all other wisdom has been flawed by folly, all other goodness has been tainted by imperfections; Jesus Christ remains the only Being of whom, without gross flattery, it could be asserted, 'He is altogether lovely.'" Belonging to

Him, we are delivered from our discredit and share His distinction.

This book similarly suggests the blessedness of...

C. Desire (Song 7:10b)

We know of the soul's longing after God as a deer pants for water (Psalm 42:1). This account is almost too sacred to repeat. Here the blessedness is not our desire for God but the bounty of His desire for us. Is this a prophetic reversal of the curse, where the wife's ruling desire was for her husband (Genesis 3:16)? Here it is the husband whose ruling desire is for the wife. The word is that God is strongly attracted to those who can say, "I am my beloved's." A powerful desire possesses God that causes Him to yearn for and stretch out after those who belong to Him. Is it possible that the all-sufficient, eternal God should have such longing for dependent, mortal man (Psalm 8:3-8)?

The truth is that God's craving for us is not that we might satisfy Him (Job 35:6-8; Proverbs 8:36a; Jeremiah 7:19; Romans 11:35). His yearning is to see how we are, and to satisfy us. He yearns after our well-being and after wholly benefiting us (Psalm 31:19; 40:5; 139:17, 18; Jeremiah 29:11; John 17:24; 1 John 4:16). Absolutely without profit on His part and altogether with benefit on ours, the eternal God desires our holiness and the holy.

The Song of love further reveals the crowning bounty of...

D. Dual Belonging

The word is not only "I am my beloved's," but also it is "my beloved is mine" (Song 6:3a). We come to the almost incredible. Belonging is not unidirectional, only our belonging to God. It is reciprocal. We belong to Him and He belongs to us. Sweeping belonging to God on our part pales before His surpassing belonging to us. We give Him ourselves as withered branches. He gives us life, fruit, and fellowship with Himself and fellow branches. In fact, in Him we have not only the gift of Himself, the true Vine and all that He is, but also all that He has (1 Corinthians 3:21-23). The language of dual belonging is not strictly stated here, but it is strongly supported. "...Ye are Christ's; and Christ is God's" (1 Corinthians 3:23); therefore Christ is yours (John 14:20). It is also strongly supported, because "all things are yours," including persons (1 Corinthians 3:21b-22a) and "ye are Christ's." Once more, therefore, Christ is yours.

In dual belonging, God in Christ does not come empty-handed, but loaded with blessed love gifts. This will be the subject of the next chapter, but it is fitting that we now highlight the unique bounty of dual belonging. Individually, each saint belongs to Christ (1 Corinthians 7:22). Individually, each receives blessings from God (Romans 11:35-36a; Ephesians 4:7; Luke 15:25-31).

The depth of the bounty of this dual belonging, however, lies in the saints' collective belonging to Christ— in the fact that "ye are Christ's" (1 Corinthians 3:23a). The KJV "ye" is plural. This refers to the oneness for which Christ prayed (John 17:22).

What marvelous dual and common belonging to Christ and joint possession with Christ, where there is no proprietorship, no poverty, no pride, no partisanship; where all is ours— all things and persons, all life and death, all present and all to come; and where we possess all this but we remain possessed by (or belonging to) nothing or no one but God! There is no highest and lowest, not greatest and smallest, not biggest and littlest, for all in Christ are one and share as one.

Belonging to God has no boundaries, but oh, the blessedness!

3.4
Conclusion

BELONGING IS THE HONOURED heartbeat of the heartbeats of holiness. The whole purpose for birthing and burying is that we might belong to God and God alone. No one in right and enlightened mind rejects the rightness, reasonableness and richness of absolute belonging to God. On our part, belonging to God must be total or not at all, but no tongue can speak the triune treasure of God Himself that awaits all who totally belong to Him.

4
BLESSING
A Holiness Heartbeat

"Be ye holy; for I am holy."

"And the angel of the LORD called unto Abraham out of heaven the second time, and said, By myself have I sworn, saith the LORD, for because thou hast done this thing, and hast not withheld thy son, thine only son: that in blessing I will bless thee…" —*Genesis 22:15-17*

"Blessed be the God and Father of our Lord Jesus Christ, who hath blessed us with all spiritual blessings in heavenly places in Christ: according as he hath chosen us in him before the foundation of the world, that we should be holy…" —*Ephesians 1:3, 4*

Introduction

AGAIN WE ARE CONSIDERING that "heartbeat" has reference to what is essential to life. In previous studies we have already considered that Birthing, Burying and Belonging are heartbeats or essentials of holiness. The proposition in this study is that Blessing is essential to holiness. In the scripture portions before us now, blessing is associated with holiness. In the Genesis passage it is related in symbolical association. In the Ephesians passage, the association of holiness with blessing is substantial.

There is, of course, blessing associated with the new birth, or entrance sanctification. So much more is there blessing associated with the "new death," or entire sanctification. There was blessing for Abraham related to the birth of Isaac, a type of entrance sanctification (Genesis 12:1, 2— "I will make of thee a great nation, and I will bless thee…"). That has in it the fact that Isaac was to be born. The promise of a great nation holds in it the promise of having a son.

There was also blessing related to the offering of Isaac, a type of entire sanctification. Genesis 22:17— "…that in blessing I will bless thee, and in multiplying I will multiply thy seed as the stars of the heaven, and as the sand which is upon the sea shore..." Added to Abraham's sand-upon-the-shore blessing was his stars-in-the-sky blessing.

"Blessing" in the Ephesians passage is the good word or action of God. We may say that holiness is God's good word of the promise of the Spirit through faith (Galatians 3:14). Blessing is also the good action of the presence of the Spirit through faith (Acts 15:8, 9). In Revelation 20:6a, "Blessed" is like beatitudinal blessing. There is, of course, blessedness related to the early Beatitudes such as poverty, mourning and hunger of spirit (Matthew 5:3, 4, 6), but there is central blessedness in relation to purity of heart (Matthew 5:8).

Without ignoring the first blessing of entrance sanctification, it is the fullness of the blessing of entire sanctification that we have in focus here. We cannot presume to deal, even in this longer chapter, with all of the details of full blessing. We shall lift out some to which we are giving priority.

Because it occupies a place of commanding concern, let us begin with the blessing that we shall call a Hearty Assurance.

4.1
A Hearty Assurance

THIS IS THE BLESSING OF being sure that one is entirely sanctified. We have called it "praying through." I do not know the ecclesiastical origin of this expression. Although stated in the negative, there is one scriptural portion that rather closely reflects and could be an explanation of the expression. Lamentations 3:44— "Thou hast covered thyself with a cloud, that our prayer should not pass through." Verses later there is a cheering, positive complement to this verse. Verses 55, 56— "I called upon thy name, O LORD, out of the low dungeon. Thou hast heard my voice: hide not thine ear at my breathing, at my cry." Praying through is knowing that God heard prayer and has favourably granted the prayer request. (See Solomon's prayer, 1 Kings 9:2, 3; and Cornelius' prayer in Acts 10:30-32). Blessed moments, when God answers prayer.

Add to that 1 John 5:14— "And this is the confidence that we have in him, that, if we ask any thing according to his will, he heareth us: and if we know that he hear us, whatsoever we ask, we know that we have the petitions that we desired of him." What this seems to be saying is, when we ask in His will, we know that the listening God hears, and if we know that God hears, we know that we have. See how "hear" and "have" are linked together. Is that how you got into grace? You knew that God heard you, and *if God heard me, then I'm saved. I am entirely sanctified. He heard me.*

We have also linked hearty assurance to the witness of the Spirit. We may all agree that one consuming concern of seekers and altar workers alike is that the soul pursuing God should have, can have, and does have the assuring witness of the Spirit to being entirely sanctified. We remember that we have pointed out some practical "twos" of two crisis works of grace, such as Invitation, or the two "comes"; and Intercession, or the two prayers. In reference to hearty assurance let me suggest that we have Indication, or the two witnesses. Romans 8:16— "The Spirit itself beareth witness with our spirit, that we are the children of God."

Acts 15:8, 9— "And God, which knoweth the hearts, bare them witness, giving them the Holy Ghost, even as he did unto us; and put no difference between us and them, purifying their hearts by faith." In terms of Indication do we have here two witnesses: a witness that we become children of God, and a witness, as the disciples said, of the Pentecostal witness. Here is a twofold witness.

The big question is, What is the witness of the Spirit? In general definition, "witness" is a "declaration that confirms or makes known anything." In many instances, it is actually the same biblical word as "testimony" (Hebrews 11:5). I do not know that I have heard any in-depth treatment concerning the nature or characteristics of the witness. It seems that God has, from His Word, some helpful details concerning the witness of the Spirit.

First, then, we may note that the witness of the Spirit that gives hearty assurance is...

A. The Creator's Witness (Acts 15:8)

Witness: direct knowledge coincident with reality; announcement of the facts; a certifying.

"Bare them witness" is one word in the original. It comes from the word from which, in the ethical sense, we get the English word "martyr" — one whose witness or belief is so significant and sure that he or she pays with his life for that witness. In our legal and judicial system, witness is testimony or evidence, or the one who gives such testimony or evidence. In a court case, a chief witness is of utmost importance.

In the spiritual setting of Christian assurance, God is our witness. God, Himself, because of His involvement in and knowledge of our sanctification, authoritatively affirms the reality of this spiritual victory. In fact, we are not amiss in calling Him the Chief Witness (Romans 8:16; Acts 15:8, 9; Romans 1:9). The Romans passage adds that witness is not only testimonial evidence, but is also the person who gives such evidence, or who does the witnessing. One significant truth that comes out of this observation is that if we have God, the Witnesser, we will always have the witness.

In God's great goodness and truth, the witness of the Spirit that gives hearty assurance is also...

B. Co-Witness (Romans 8:16)

The expression "beareth witness" (also one word) is different from "bare them witness" (Acts 15:8). The word "beareth witness" in Romans 8:16 is an enlargement of the basic word by the addition of the prefix, which means "together with." In other words, it means to bear joint witness. The New Century Version carries this emphasis. It says, "And the Spirit himself joins with our spirits to say we are God's children." What we have here is God observing the ancient principle that two or three witnesses establish truth, Deuteronomy 19:15— "One witness shall not rise up against a man for any iniquity, or for any sin, in any sin that he sinneth: at the mouth of two witnesses, or at the mouth of three witnesses, shall the matter be established." Jesus not only maintained this principle but also God, in Christ, upholds and honours this great principle of verified witness (John 8:13, 17, 18). So it is, here, God allows us and calls upon us to join Him in confirming the sanctifying work in our own hearts. What an honour and responsibility this is!

If this concept is new to us in the spiritual realm, we need to remember that it functions in the social sphere. At their marriage, couples themselves form a very significant part of the major group of witnesses to their marriage. Similarly, the Scriptures are indeed saying that we ourselves are joint witnesses with God to the transaction of spiritual victory. 1 John 5:10— "He that believeth on the Son of God hath the witness in himself." We need reverently to accept that witness to entire sanctification is ours as well as God's.

All this means that it is absolutely vital to know what we are to do, and what we are doing, and what we have done, when we come seeking fully to be God's and to have God in His fullness. My own testimony is that as I have come to a clearer understanding of burying and belonging, my assurance of my being God's and His being mine has become more pronounced and more precious.

We may go a step further to note that witness is...

C. Central Witness

The Scriptures make it clear where the source of witness resides. The Book of Acts states that witness involves the "heart" (Acts 15:8). Heart, as used here, denotes the inward center of spiritual life. The Epistle to the Romans locates witness in the "spirit" (Romans 8:16). The spirit is the immaterial center of contact with God. "God is a Spirit..." (John 4:24). He has made man as spirit and body (1 Thessalonians 5:23). It is not, however, in the body that God bears witness but in the spirit. We need to bear in mind that spirit hears without ears or physical sounds; sees without eyes or physical light; thinks and feels without nerves or physical brains; speaks without lips or verbal symbols. Spirit is spiritual and is fundamentally volitional rather than physically sensational.

The witness, therefore, takes place in the central and essential being of man rather than in the circumferential and emotional boundaries of man. Witness, therefore, is not so much a physical feeling as it is a spiritual fact; not so much physical sensation as it is spiritual substance. Like Elijah, we reach after some wind, earthquake or fire emotion, but God essentially speaks in expression with still, small voice.

1 Kings 19:9-13— "And he came thither unto a cave, and lodged there; and, behold, the word of the LORD came to him, and he said unto him, What doest thou here, Elijah? And he said, I have been very jealous for the LORD God of hosts: for the children of Israel have forsaken thy covenant, thrown down thine altars, and slain thy prophets with the sword; and I, even I only, am left; and they seek my life, to take it away. And he said, Go forth, and stand upon the mount before the LORD. And, behold, the LORD passed by, and a great and strong wind rent the mountains, and brake in pieces the rocks before the LORD; but the LORD was not in the wind: and after the wind an earthquake; but the LORD was not in the earthquake: and after the earthquake a fire; but the LORD was not in the fire: and after the fire a still small voice." They tell me this translates into "the sound of a stillness." And God came.

Further, witness is...

D. A Common Witness

Dispositional accompaniments of the witness may differ. Some speak of a sense of being flooded with love, with joy, or with peace. Some shout, some spring, others sing. However different the accompaniments are, the anchorage is the same. God, Who is Spirit, always witnesses to our spirit, and always wants the confirming, common witness of our own spirits.

None, then, ought to feel that he needs to have another person's accompaniments, or has to impose his accompaniments on another. We may remember the blind men to whom Jesus restored sight in three different ways. One man's sight came after mud-anointing and washing (John 9:5-7). For two sets of twos, sight came after touching (Matthew 9:27-30a; 20:30-34).

In a third case, that of the well-known Bartimaeus, there was neither anointing nor touching (Mark 10:46-52). In each case the common denominator was the act of seeing rather than the accompaniments of seeing. So in things spiritual, the common ground of witness is that it is the Creator's Witness. It is Co-Witness, and it is Central Witness to a common work.

Some may find themselves saying that all this about the Creator's witness, co-witness and central witness is good. But still, what about unshakable assurance? We can and need to say, then, that witness is very definitely...

E. Certain Witness

In dealing with the witness of the spirit, we are focusing on events that are essentially spiritual rather than physical. For this very reason we need to recognize and remember the biblical truth that the things that are seen are temporal and passing, while the things that are not seen are eternal and permanent (2 Corinthians 4:18b). We need, therefore, to disabuse our minds of the false acceptance that physical phenomena are more certain than the spiritual. In fact, it is just the opposite.

Let us then consider some spiritual elements related to assurance of the witness of the spirit. There is first the certainty of what we may call,

1. Our Spiritual Foundation

The foundation of sanctification and the certainty of the witness of the spirit rests firmly on the foundation of the One Who sanctified Himself that we might be sanctified (John 17:19). Jesus is the holy One, Who had a holy birth, lived a holy life, died a holy death, demonstrated a holy resurrection, had a holy ascension, occupies the holy position at His Father's right hand, and this very moment offers holy intercession for all the world of individuals who need His holy atonement (Acts 13:26-39; Romans 8:31-34).

With Edward Mote (1834), who gave us the words, and William B. Bradbury (1863), who gave us the music, we must justly exult:

> My hope is built on nothing less
> > Than Jesus' blood and righteousness.
> I dare not trust the sweetest frame,
> > But wholly lean on Jesus' name.
>
> When darkness seems to hide His face,
> > I rest on His unchanging grace.
> In every high and stormy gale,
> > My anchor holds within the veil.
>
> His oath, His covenant, His blood,
> > Support me in the whelming flood.
> When all around my soul gives way,
> > He then is all my Hope and Stay.
>
> On Christ, the solid Rock, I stand;
> All other ground is sinking sand.

There is this unshakable certainty of our firm Foundation, but there is also the certainty of,

2. Some Spiritual Facts

We may mention the three important sets of facts that pre-date blessing. Each has the basis of definite spiritual knowing.

There are first,

a. The Facts of Spiritual Birthing

Romans 6:3, 4— "Know ye not, that so many of us as were baptized into Jesus Christ were baptized into his death? Therefore we are buried with him by baptism into death: that like as Christ was raised up from the dead by the glory of the Father, even so we also should walk in newness of life."

"Knowing" in verse 3 relates to "the mind, comprising alike the faculties of perceiving and understanding and those of feeling, judging, determining." It is a combination of mental examination and personal experience, and refers to "the power of considering and judging soberly, calmly and impartially."

We fully understand that the "newness" of birthing (verse 4c) is not chronological but character newness. We fully understand that new-birth life is like "the absolute fullness of life, both essential and ethical, which belongs to God." We understand fully also that new-birth life is "real and genuine, a life active and vigorous, devoted to God, blessed, in the portion even in this world of those who put their trust in Christ." We can know, beyond shadow of doubt, these facts related to spiritual birthing.

There are, next,

b. The Facts of Spiritual Burying

Romans 6:5-7— "For if we have been planted together in the likeness of his death, we shall be also in the likeness of his resurrection: knowing this, that our old man is crucified with him, that the body of sin might be destroyed, that henceforth we should not serve sin. For he that is dead is freed from sin."

It is interesting that "knowing" in verse 6 is "knowledge grounded on personal experience." We can come personally and practically to the real meat of Frances R. Havergal's great hymn of consecration. We can know that we have done more than give to God "moments and… days," "hands and… feet," "voice and… lips," "silver and… gold—(and) intellect." We may know that we have complied with the depth of giving, having said to God, and meant it,

> Take my will and make it Thine;
> It shall be no longer mine.
> Take my heart; it is thine own!
> It shall be Thy royal [maybe better, humble] throne.
>
> Take my love; my God, I pour
> At Thy feet its treasure store.
> Take myself and I will be
> Ever, only, all for Thee.

As well as, or even better than, married persons know that they have made the marriage commitment, we can know that we have had the "planted" experience with Christ (Romans 6:5). We can know that we have let go ourselves, like a living seed, to fall into the ground and die (John 12:24). We can know, beyond shadow of doubt, these facts related to spiritual burying.

Then there are also,

c. The Facts of Spiritual Belonging

Romans 6:8-11— "Now if we be dead with Christ, we believe that we shall also live with him: knowing that Christ being raised from the dead dieth no more; death hath no more dominion over him. For in that he died, he died unto sin once: but in that he liveth, he liveth unto God. Likewise reckon ye also yourselves to be dead indeed unto sin, but alive unto God through Jesus Christ our Lord."

"Knowing" here (verse 9) is to have clear mental perception, and therefore to cherish "the force and meaning" of the fact that crucifixion with Christ effectively ends our former relationship with the devilishness of the sin of self-divinity (verses 6 and 11a). It is also to have clear mental perception, and therefore to cherish "the force and meaning" of the fact that since crucifixion with Christ fully terminated, by death, relationship with the old body of carnal self-divinity, then on those grounds, and those alone, we belong to Christ and Christ belongs to us (Romans 6:11b; 7:1-4).

Knowing, beyond shadow of doubt, these facts related to spiritual Birthing, Burying, Belonging, we graciously become absolutely certain and accepted co-witnesses with the Holy Spirit.

There is, however, not only the certainty that comes from our Spiritual Foundation and Spiritual Facts, there is also the certainty that comes from,

3. Spiritual Faith

Spiritual faith belongs to the realm of the non-visual eternal. We cannot see nor touch faith, but it is nonetheless vitally real. In the realm of the eternal, faith is proven substance (Hebrews 1:1-3). The faith that brings certainty is not faith in a false, self-created, lashing, limiting and tarnished God. It is faith in the faithful, uncreated, living and loving true God (Hebrews 11:6). It is the open door of God for all, whatever the state or station, to have access to Him.

I see more and more that I have become too anxious about exercising faith, and then more and more agonized because I did not seem to be entering into faith. Now I understand more and more that, at least for myself, it is more possible to come to believing God for His fullness in me, when I concentrate primarily on bringing my fullness to God. The more I submit to how radical must be my giving myself to God, the more I sense how real is God's giving Himself to me. For some of us, obeying faith is obtaining faith (Hebrews 11:4-8).

Spiritual faith, then, certainly operates almost automatically when it is accompanied by the truth about our Spiritual Foundation and the Spiritual Facts of Birthing, Burying and Belonging (1 John 1:9).

There is one other word about witness that is profitable to consider. Witness is...

F. Comprehensive Witness

The plan of God in giving assurance through witness is evidently purposely designed to give two-fold assurance.

Comprehensive witness therefore includes,

1. Crisis Witness

The tense of the verb "bare them witness" in Acts 15:8 is the Greek tense that indicates to holiness theologians the concept and reality that a crisis witness occurs at the very moment of crisis victory. We would have a special appreciation of this type of hearty assurance. Crisis witness is obviously of great importance to the certainty of when victory came. It may likely be helpful, though in a lesser sense, that crisis witness marks where it came. The importance, really, is that victory has come. Not recognizing that witness is always common witness, some would even make too much of the accompaniments of crisis witness. I heard one dear Christian gentleman testify that his crisis witness of the Spirit came with shouting, and that every once in a while he needs to have a "shouting spell" to keep the witness and the victory fresh and vital. The truth is that we do not need to make a shrine out of crisis victory. It may be even dangerous, or at least distressing, to assurance to believe that we must have repetitions of crisis witness.

Addressing this concern is the observation that God has evidently designed comprehensive witness to include,

2. Continual Witness

Whereas the tense of the verb "bare them witness" in Acts 15:8 is the tense that highlights crisis witness, the Greek tense of the verb "beareth witness" is the tense that heralds continuing witness. The good news is that as the abundant presence of the Holy Spirit precipitates crisis witness, so His abiding presence perpetuates constant witness. There is really no need to feel under obligation to have crisis witness repeated. One of the glories of entire sanctification is that the abiding Witnesser provides abiding witness both to His presence and to His purity in our hearts and lives.

We have seen that assurance is solidly founded on the Creator's Witness, Co-Witness, Central Witness, Common Witness, Certain Witness, and Comprehensive Witness. Hearty Assurance is indeed one of the wonderful blessings of initial, and well as of intensive, holiness.

Another blessing of holiness is the blessing of Heavenly Affections.

4.2
Heavenly Affections

THE BIBLE MAKES IT CLEAR that it is the fallen flesh that manifests a life of moral corruption (Galatians 5:19-21). Similarly it is the Satanic self-sovereignty of carnality that gives rise to competition and contention (1 Corinthians 3:3-7). The self-surrendered and the Spirit-filled are Christlike (Ephesians 5:18-21; Galatians 5:22-26). Incidentally, we have here another example of distinction between entrance and entire sanctification, or between initial and intensive holiness. From the standpoint of Increase, the Bible presents two groups of affections or fruits of the Spirit. Ephesians 5:9— "…for the fruit of the Spirit is in all goodness and righteousness and truth…"

Those fruits are very typical of our lives when we have just been born again. The "goodness" means that we have such a zeal for goodness that we manifest it in correcting others without mellowness. "Righteousness" is a careful conformity to all the standards. We walk on needles and pins when we are born again, we are so concerned about all the standards. "Truth" means we have such a love for reality that we have no interest in artificiality. Aren't those good, born again traits?

But when we come over to Galatians 5 we have an entirely different list of fruits. In terms of increase the entrance sanctification fruits are the fruits which manifest a lack of maturity, a little bit of severity, legality. But when we come to the entire sanctification fruits it's different. Our focus is on the heavenly affections or fruits of the entirely sanctified.

These fruits clearly are...

A. The Father's Fruits (Galatians 5:22)

Spiritual fruits, either on the level of initial holiness or intensive holiness, come only from God the Holy Spirit (Ephesians 5:9; Galatians 5:22, 23). At the same time Jesus speaks not only of the fruits of the corrupt but also of the good as being "their fruits" (Matthew 7:17-20). This reflects one of the mysteries and mercies of redemption. In relation to fruit bearing, only in living a life crucified with Christ do Christians manifest the fruits of holiness that have their source only in Christ (Galatians 2:20). The secret is surrendering to be Christlike in character, rather than struggling to be correct in conduct.

What fills us characterizes how we function. Those filled with wine act like drunkards (Ephesians 5:18). Those filled with Satan act like the Devil (John 8:44). Those occupied with some of the Spirit, some of self, act like the double-minded (James 4:8). On the other hand, those filled with the Spirit act like the Divine (Ephesians 5:18b-21).

The fruits of heavenly affections, being the Father's fruits, are of course...

B. The Finest Fruit (Galatians 5:22, 23)

One view is that unlike the gifts of the Spirit, the fruit of the Spirit form a collective whole. We may therefore speak of the collection in the singular as "fruit." While no believer possesses all of the gifts, each is to possess the entire nine virtues that make up the fruit as a group.

Love, here, is the unconditional, unconquerable love of God. Love that turns to hate is emotional, not eternal love. Love that leaks out is lesser love, not the Lord's love. All blessed with the Spirit's love, love God exclusively, and neighbours and self inclusively (Matthew 22:36-40; Mark 12:30, 31). They also love enemies Christlikely (Matthew 5:43-48). They love, in fact, not because others are loveable, but because they are love.

Joy is rejoicing that is not based on the good things of life but on the grace of the Lord. All who possess the Spirit's joy have a gladness whose source is copious and continuous and exclusively in Christ (John 15:11).

Peace is the deep, undisturbed rest that is the result of reconciled and radical relationship with God through redemption. It is the end not necessarily of earthly, external suffering, but of internal strife. All who possess the Spirit's peace have an untroubled, undisturbed and unceasing rest that comes from belonging exclusively to Christ. He says, "Peace I leave with you, my peace I give unto you: not as the world giveth, give I unto you" (John 14:27). His is a special peace that remains even when there is turmoil.

Longsuffering is patience with persons. All who possess the Spirit's longsuffering have a patience that has the controlled power of revenge, and therefore do not use it. They have a patience that springs from love, that works, withstands and waits in the hope of winning others to God and goodness (1 Corinthians 13:4a).

Gentleness is not gutlessness but graciousness. All who possess the Spirit's gentleness have grace that pervades the whole nature, mellowing all that is sharp and severe, and that manifests being helpful rather than harsh. Those who know God's gentleness have a composure and strength that make them and others great (Psalm 18:35).

GOODNESS is the twin grace of gentleness. All who possess the Spirit's goodness have the ability to minister correction without harshness and losing gentleness (Ephesians 5:8).

FAITH is faithfulness, constancy, loyalty, steadfastness and steadiness in relationship with God and others.

MEEKNESS is not mushiness but manliness (or womanliness). All who possess the Spirit's meekness are big and therefore can be little; great and therefore can be taught; strong and therefore can be weak. Meekness gives such height in God that its possessors are humble.

All who possess the Spirit's TEMPERANCE live out of the strength of God, and out of strength in God that produces self-discipline in all of life's desires, drives and doings.

These heavenly affections constitute not just lovely literature. They call for lovelier living. As a blessing of holiness, it is a reality to possess these fruits of the Spirit and to portray, on earth, God's blessed and beautiful behaviour.

There is crucial need for us to consider, however briefly, a very needy blessing of holiness. It is the blessing of Holy Authority.

4.3
Holy Authority

Acts 1:8— "But ye shall receive power, after that the Holy Ghost is come upon you: and ye shall be witnesses unto me both in Jerusalem, and in all Judæa, and in Samaria, and unto the uttermost part of the earth."

THE LITERAL EXPRESSION IS "the power of the Holy Ghost coming on you." Power is inherent (built in, constitutional). The word family from which power comes carries the meaning of ability, capability and authority.

When the gospel came into the world, there existed nothing but a mockery of authority. The Greeks, though they continued to have language and other influences, lost authority in national slavery. The Romans had no real authority, only cruelty and brutality. There was no limit, for instance, to Roman legal beatings. When they beat Jesus it went on and on and on. When they would beat criminals they were really trying to beat them to death. Some people get the impression that cruelty and brutality is authority, but it isn't. It is nothing more than littleness and weakness and inferiority. Even the Jews themselves, God's special people, had lost authority. The religious leaders lost authority by their secularity— being more interested in praise and profit rather than purity (Matthew 6:1-5; Mark 7:6, 7, 10-12); the Pharisees, by their hypocrisy (Matthew 23:13-33); and the Sadducees, by their unwholesome liberalism (Matthew 22:23-30).

In our day the need for holy authority is even more critical. Generally speaking, politicians have lost authority by their corruptibility; educators, by their human rationality; the media, by its partiality; the rich and the professionals, by their rapacity.

Parents, too, have lost authority because of their unchristian individuality and carnality. One of the problems of parenting is that *I want to live as an individual, and I don't want to be bothered with some little people tying up my individuality.* Once you become a parent, you have to give up a lot of individuality to minister to others. So we lose our authority because we become individualistic. Even the Church has lost authority by its insipidity and loss of brilliancy (Matthew 5:13-16).

The problem is that each group and person is concerned about furthering only personal advantage.

The answer to the deplorable need for authority is the same now as it has always been. The world needs a new demonstration of...

A. Mighty Authority

This kind of authority comes exclusively from and through the absolutely holy God.

God dispensed His authority through,

1. The Incarnate and Only Christ

One of the great and refreshing characteristics of Christ was that into an abominable world, He came as the absolute Way with the authentic wisdom (John 14:6; Matthew 7:28, 29).

God also dispensed authority through,

2. The Indwelling and Other Comforter (John 16:7-11)

When the Holy Spirit, the Comforter, came to indwell the disciples in all of His fullness, He turned horrible holocaust of life before Pentecost into productive Pentecost; and the fearful into the fearless and the fruitful (Acts 1:8; 2:1-41). Previously doubting disciples, full of dread, became dynamic doers and declarers of the news of redemption through the risen Christ. They testified promptly and clearly that power other than their own was responsible for their redemptive results (Acts 3:1-12, 16). The only answer to their complete change was the Mighty Authority of Christ's Other Comforter.

The Mighty Authority of God was transformed to work in the disciples and in us as...

B. Moral Authority

Moral authority is authority that came not only from the purity of the disciples' lives but also from divine partnership in their labours.

Theirs was the moral authority of,

1. Obvious, Cleansed Christians

Their lips voiced this cleansing (Acts 15:8). More than this, their lives verified this cleansing. In the mighty moment of their Pentecostal blessing, God cleansed from their hearts and lives the carnal dispute, disagreements and open displeasure that had before divided them. These men, and the movement of persons God was raising up through them, were again and again characterized by glorious unity (Acts 2:46; 4:24, 32; 5:12). Indeed, before Pentecost, the disciples were midget men who did all in their power to save their lives (Mark 14:50). After Pentecost these same men became mighty martyrs who were not afraid of doing the things that would lead even to sacrificing their lives (Acts 4:17-20).

The moral authority of the disciples was also that of,

2. Observable Christ Companions

Acts 4:13— "Now when they saw the boldness of Peter and John, and perceived that they were unlearned and ignorant men, they marvelled; and they took knowledge of them, that they had been with Jesus."

God used the disciples to heal the impotent man at the temple gate. The context uses two words for "whole" (verses 9 and 10). These words suggest that the man received complete healing, spiritual as well as physical. About God's agents to bring healing, "The Greek literally says that Peter and John were 'unlettered' and 'uninstructed.'" This means that the disciples were "uneducated in the technical, rabbinical teachings. They were commoners in that they possessed no official positions nor special abilities."

The Believers Study Bible observes as follows: "The outstanding thing the high priest and those who were with him could remember about these men was 'that they had been with Jesus.'" It then ends with the powerful comment that their companionship with Christ "was their credential for extraordinary power."

What this indicates is that the mighty authority that is always God's can be moral authority in us and through us. To make this clear God specializes in blessing with moral authority,

3. Odd, Chosen Conquerors

1 Corinthians 1:26-31— "For ye see your calling, brethren, how that not many wise men after the flesh, not many mighty, not many noble, are called: but God hath chosen the foolish things of the world to confound the wise; and God hath chosen the weak things of the world to confound the things which are mighty; and base things

of the world, and things which are despised, hath God chosen, yea, and things which are not, to bring to nought things that are: that no flesh should glory in his presence. But of him are ye in Christ Jesus, who of God is made unto us wisdom, and righteousness, and sanctification, and redemption: that, according as it is written, He that glorieth, let him glory in the Lord."

Do you see what is open to us? The more helpless we will admit that we are, and the more we go to God in faith, the more God is able to manifest His marvelous power and glory through our lives. It is amazing what God will do through any life that is wholly God's.

The application of all of this to us is that in our world, more sadly lost spiritually because it is so gravely lost ethically and morally, we need to go beyond emphasizing heavenly affections and also urgently entreat for a revival of holy authority that is equally a blessing of holiness.

The last of the blessings that we will consider in this study is really the first and the basic blessing. I have left it for last for two reasons. First, I sense the conviction that one of our problems is that, at least in practical living if not in doctrinal understanding, we do not have an adequate focus of this blessing. The other reason is that I wished to leave the need for this blessing prominent in our hearts and minds.

I am referring to the blessing of what I am calling the High Almighty.

4.4
The High Almighty

ISAIAH 57:15 TALKS ABOUT GOD being the "high and lofty One that inhabiteth eternity," but He also dwells in the humble and holy heart. The reigning God in His high and holy heaven is also the residing God in humble and holy hearts.

There are two words for "blessing" in the scriptures. This is confirmed by the fact that while blessing in Ephesians 1:3, 4 is in reference to the external, good action of God, blessing in Revelation 20:6 (as in the Beatitudes) has reference to the internal, great abiding of God. He fully satisfies those He indwells. We may add, He also makes us fully sufficient and fruitfully serving because He is fully sovereign and settled in our spirits.

Our basic and best blessing is indeed the High Almighty in...

A. The Person, God.

It is true that God is a Spirit, but He is the creating, talking Person, Who can be worshiped and adored, and Who is Father and seeks our reverent relationship (John 4:23, 24). Jesus and the Father are one (John 10:30). He is very God, the Person Who, though God, became man. He came. He lived on earth. He died for our sins. He rose again. He now lives forever at His Father's right hand, ever to make intercession for us (Philippians 2:5-11; Romans 8:34). God the Holy Spirit is the divine Person. He is not an influence or an It, but the ever-near and abiding Comforter (John 15:26).

All of this is enriched when we reflect that God is,

1. The True Person

John 17:3a— "And this is life eternal, that they might know thee the only true God…"

"True" means that as Jesus is the only genuine Vine (John 15:1), God is the only genuine God (2 Kings 19:15-19). It means that all other so-called gods are false and therefore failing. Our God only is the real, relational, reliable and renowned God. Zechariah 14 begins in verse 1 with, "Behold, the day of the LORD cometh…" Every little John and Susie has their day, but one of these days, it's going to be God's day. *O God, let every day be Your day. I don't want to wait.* Look at verse 4: "…his feet shall stand in that day upon the mount of Olives…"

Look at verse 6: "And it shall come to pass in that day, that the light shall not be clear, nor dark: but … at evening time it shall be light."

Look at verse 8: "And it shall be in that day, that living waters shall go out from Jerusalem…"

Look at verse 9: "And the LORD shall be king over all the earth: in that day shall there be one LORD…"

Verse 13: "And it shall come to pass in that day, that a great tumult from the LORD shall be among them…"

God is going to come and stop all the proud speeches of men. It is going to be God's day one of these days. He is the True God.

The Person, God, is,

2. The Triune Person (Matthew 28:19; 2 Corinthians 13:14)

We have in the blessing of the Person of God, the unique God Who is Trinity and yet unity, or one God (Zechariah 14:9; Mark 12:29). God has seemed to reveal one insight into the mystery of the Trinity as one God. God is holy, and one meaning of holy is belonging. Because, therefore, God is holy, He is also Trinity, for one person does not represent relationship.

In my travels I met a Christian young man who reads widely and is a serious student of philosophical thought. What a joy it was to talk with him about the deep things of God. In one of our conversations he shared the knowledge that at least three persons are necessary to reflect unselfish relationship.

Ecclesiastes 4:8-12— "There is one alone, and there is not a second; yea, he hath neither child nor brother: yet is there no end of all his labour; neither is his eye satisfied with riches; neither saith he, For whom do I labour, and bereave my soul of good? This is also vanity… Two are better than one; because they have a good reward for their labour. For if they fall, the one will lift up his fellow… And if one prevail against him, two shall withstand him; and a threefold cord is not quickly broken."

God says, one doesn't really work very well; two, great; but a threefold cord… Isn't it true that, even though husband and wife are two, we really need a third Person to make marriage work?

Earthly twos need God to make them successful teams of three. God the Father is the Excelsior of life and salvation. God the Son is the Example and Expiator of life and salvation. God the Holy Spirit is the Executive of life and salvation. The revelation is that our God only is the relational God, that the three Persons in the godhood are so absolutely related that the Three are uniquely, only One God, and that the Triune God shares intimate relationship with each of the entirely sanctified.

The Person, God, is also,

3. The Trustworthy Person
God is trustworthy because He is the unchanging Person (Malachi 3:6a; Hebrews 13:8). God is trustworthy because He is the unfailing Person (1 Kings 8:56).

Furthermore, the Person, God, is,

4. The Tender Person
The Psalms are full of the tender mercies of God (Psalm 25:6). His tender mercies are similar to His Fatherly pity (Psalm 103:13).

Our problem is that as persons defiled, deceived and destroyed by the rebellious, self-sovereign "I," we have become not only our own false gods, but we have created a false concept of the Triune God. We see God the Father as unfeeling, unfriendly, far away, flogging, fearful, frowning.

That is one reason why Jesus came to show us the Father (John 14:7-9). The Father is just like Jesus— friendly, fair, forgiving, favouring, folding, feeding, feeling; and flogging, yes, but for forming; not forsaking but fashioning (Hebrews 12:5-10). So it is also that fallen man, creating a false image of God the Holy Spirit, sees the Spirit as magical, manipulating and even monstrous. Jesus also reveals the nature of the Holy Spirit (John 14:16). Like Jesus, the Other Comforter is man-understanding, mindful, ministering, and full of mercy.

The root blessing of the High Almighty is not only in the Person of God, but also in...

B. The Presence of God

His presence is,

1. Living Presence (Matthew 16:16)
"Living" does not describe biological life that is merely reproducing life, but rather spiritual life that is regenerating life.

God's presence is,

2. Loving Presence (John 17:23b)
Part of amazing grace is that God loves us with unspeakable love that is divine and completely independent love (John 3:16). He loves even when we were a part of this wayward world. He also, however, loves with devoted, common interest love (John 16:27a). He loves the partially loveable in us till He can bring us to the perfectly loveable (John 21:15-17).

His presence is also,

3. Longing Presence (Song 7:10; Genesis 4:7ab)
Sin longs to soil, strip and subdue us, but God longs far more to save, to sanctify and to be sovereign Lover in us.

His crowning presence is,

4. Lasting Presence (John 14:16-18)
Simply put, God is not a running-off-and-leaving-us God! When He comes He comes to abide. Our problem is that we believe in backsliding, and we practice it so readily. We believe that God is a God that jumps in and out of us. If you balled up your fist and put it under the nose of God, and told Him to go, He would politely take His departure.

But if you foul up, do some foolishness, the Lord is just waiting to reveal the foolishness to you, and say, *Friend, I have been here all the time, waiting.* It is not easy to backslide; there is a God Who has come to abide.

4.5
Conclusion

THERE SEEMS GREAT NEED TO appreciate and to apply that there are no blessings apart from God Himself, the Blesser, Who is the blessed God (1 Timothy 1:11). Let us be more concerned about God's presence than about God's presents. Too cheaply we tend to think of the blessings of God in terms of the presents of Hearty Assurance, Heavenly Affections, and Holy Authority that He gives. The presents are really secondary. We need to reflect, with reverence and rejoicing, that God the Person— the true, the triune, the trustworthy, the tender Person— is Himself His primary and priority present to us and in us.

This means that if we have God the Blesser and He has us, we will have the gift of blessings. If we have God the Witnesser and He has us, we will have the gift of the Hearty Assurance that comes through the witness of the Spirit. If we have God the Holy One and Sanctifier and He has us, we will have the gift of Heavenly Affections. If we have God the authoritative One and He has us, we will have the gift of holy Authority.

By extension, if we have God the Lover and He has us, we will have the gift of love. If we have God the Joy Giver and He has us, we will have the gift of joy. If we have God the Prince of Peace and He has us, we will have the gift of peace. If we have God the Teacher and He has us, we will have the gift of teaching. If we have God the Revealer and He has us, we will have the gift of revelation. If we have God the Comforter (Who is the Helper) and He has us, we will have gifts of comfort and help. If we have God the Stabilizer and He has us, we will have the gift of stability.

We could go on and on. In short, if we have God the Giver and He has us, we shall have His gifts.

A rich father purposed to give his entire estate to his reliable and trusted servant. The one exception was that he would give one gift only to his rebellious son. The son gave the matter great thought and then said that he would ask for the servant as His request.

Spiritually, of course, we could not have the righteous, reliable and trusted Servant without being changed into His reliability and trustworthiness (1 John 5:11-12). So then, if we have the Person of God the Giver, Who is the source of blessing, we will have the presents or gifts. The Person and His presents, the Giver and His gifts will then become our sure course of blessing to others.

We need and should have Hearty Assurance, Heavenly Affections, and Holy Authority. We need and should want, however, not only these blessings, but also, first, the greatest blessing— the Blesser Who loves and seeks, saves and keeps, cleanses and fuses, dresses and blesses, and satisfies and uses the soul.

Let us take God in our lives.

5
BECOMING
A Holiness Heartbeat

"Be ye holy; for I am holy."

"Wherefore gird up the loins of your mind, be sober, and hope to the end for the grace that is to be brought unto you at the revelation of Jesus Christ; as obedient children, not fashioning yourselves according to the former lusts in your ignorance: but as he which hath called you is holy, so be ye holy in all manner of conversation; because it is written, Be ye holy; for I am holy." —*1 Peter 1:13-16*

Introduction

IN THIS FINAL STUDY of holiness heartbeats, we repeat that heartbeat has reference to what is essential to life. Becoming has reference to continuation and growth in holiness. The proposition, therefore, is that becoming, or continuation and growth, is essential to holiness.

Over and over, again and again, I have clearly articulated and scripturally indicated or illustrated why I am fully persuaded that there are two crisis works of grace. We have called the first, entrance sanctification. We do so since our study on Birthing, a heartbeat of holiness, established that holiness begins in the new birth. It is a complete and finished work of grace, hence a crisis. John 3:3— "...Except a man be born again..." The Greek tense of the verb points to the fact that one is not forever borning— being born. The second crisis work of grace is entire sanctification. This is also a complete and finished work of grace, hence a crisis. John 12:24— "Verily, verily, I say unto you, Except a corn of wheat fall into the ground..." We have the same kind of verb: "fall." It happens. The Greek tense of the verb here also points to the fact that the seed is not forever falling.

When we speak, therefore, of becoming as a heartbeat of holiness, we are definitely not speaking of a continual growth in initial holiness that has no base in a crisis grace of intensive holiness.

Let us, again, honestly recognize that movements that have taught and practiced two crisis works of grace have generally emphasized saintliness of behaviour, and not also set-apartness of belonging. We need also to recognize that while such movements have rightly majored on the crisis of getting entirely sanctified, they have marginalized continuation, or growing in entire sanctification. I am fully persuaded in my own heart that becoming, growing, or continuing — especially following crisis entire sanctification — is a vital heartbeat of holiness.

One of the things that we must understand, in coming to grips with becoming, is to look at it from the standpoint of Paradoxical Truth.

5.1
Paradoxical Truth

Paradoxical truth definitely supports becoming as a part of the life of holiness. It may seem contrary to common sense that if entire sanctification, for example, is a complete work of grace that takes place in a moment, how then can there be need or room for completing what is complete, or perfecting what is perfect?

It does so because it points to the difference between...

A. Perfection and Purity

"Perfection" is not the same as "purity." Perfection is not a member of the holiness word family. Purity is (1 Timothy 4:12).

The difference between perfection and purity has become apparent because,

1. Perfection is Always a Process

If I am correct, as a layman trying to use helps to understanding Greek, it appears to me the holiness movement does err when it makes Christian perfection to be the same as entire sanctification.

There are two major New Testament words used for perfect and perfecting. One emphasizes spiritual adulthood or other moral accomplishment (Colossians 1:28; James 1:4). The other has to do with spiritual adapting or other mental adjustment (2 Corinthians 13:11). Each of these usages is related to process, or becoming, that is in progress (Hebrews 6:1— adulthood; 2 Corinthians 13:9— adjustment).

Ephesians 4:11, 12— "And he gave some, apostles; and some, prophets; and some, evangelists; and some, pastors and teachers; for the perfecting of the saints..." There is a lot of mental adjustment that we need, even after the crisis, to help us along in our Christian experience. That is why we so much need the preaching of the Word of God in the day in which we live.

Each may also be related to process that has arrived at its goal (Hebrews 7:11— adulthood; Ephesians 4:12— adjustment). Both words, however, always involve process, becoming, or continuation, and never crisis. One scholar says that the process may reach its goal, either in spiritual adulthood or in spiritual adjustment, but it is process. In addition, both of the applications of perfection are given, not as synonyms for holiness, but as supplements to sanctification (2 Corinthians 7:1— adulthood; Ephesians 4:12— adjustment).

When it comes to entire sanctification, one of the big planks of our doctrine is that it is crisis. If perfecting and perfection is always related to process, and if entire sanctification deals with crisis, then how can process be called crisis?

In contrast to perfection, however,

2. Purity is Often a Crisis

The verb form of purity is, of course, purify. Even in reference to the Old Testament ceremonies, an act of purifying is given in that Greek tense that is sometimes used to represent decisive and definite action (John 11:55; Acts 21:24). In the New Testament, there is a similar instance relating an act of purification (James 4:8). Like purity, sanctification belongs to the holiness word family, and its verb form is, of course, sanctify. When Jesus prays that His disciples should be sanctified by the truth, the verb tense of "sanctify" is that tense, in the original language, that represents decisive and definite action (John 17:17). The same tense obtains in other passages of scripture (Ephesians 5:26; Hebrews 13:12; 1 Peter 3:15).

In addition, we need to note that "sanctification" itself (or purification) supports both the concept of crisis and continuation, or becoming. In terms of the Greek tense, there is what we may call a "lightening" sanctification that is naturally a crisis. Ephesians 5:25, 26— "Husbands, love your wives, even as Christ also loved the church, and gave himself for it; that he might sanctify… it…" Again the tense is, it happens. So sanctification is, thank God, a crisis. There some people who would like to tell us sanctification is always process. No. The Word of God says entire sanctification is crisis.

There is also present tense, lifelong sanctification that is a necessary continuation (Hebrews 2:11). Becoming or continuation is therefore applicable both to purity or sanctification and to perfection, but crisis is never applicable to perfection.

It appears, therefore, that because perfection is always a process and purity is often a crisis, Christian perfection is not the parallel of crisis sanctification, but rather the perfecting of it. The holiness movement rightly emphasizes the crisis nature of entrance and of entire sanctification. It would therefore seem more accurate not to equate Christian perfection with entire sanctification, but to see perfection as an added necessity for becoming to be a heartbeat of holiness.

We need to bear in mind, however, that not to have

a crisis work that completely cleanses from the inbred, Adamic nature of attempted self-divinity, and yet strive to attain holiness following entrance sanctification only by progression or becoming, is contrary to the scriptures and is to try to build a house of holiness on the sandy foundation of selfish self. There can be no standing in the storm. To put it another way, to try continual becoming without crisis burying is not in accordance with scriptural truth but is a work of vanity and not a way to victory.

Sanctification is also process. Hebrews 2:11— "For both he that sanctifieth [that word means both he that keeps on sanctifying] and they who are [being] sanctified are all of one: for which cause he is not ashamed to call them brethren..." I believe God gets too ashamed of some of us Christians, because we are not *being* sanctified. We are not becoming, and in our not becoming we bring Him so much heartache.

So there is a sense in which sanctification is a crisis, and there is a sense in which it is continuation.

Paradoxical truth further strongly supports becoming as a call to holiness because it points to the difference between...

B. Falling Accidentally and Falling Away

We recognize that there are among Christians differences in doctrine. There are people who look at us and say, *You believe in Christian perfection. You believe in entire sanctification as a crisis work of grace. You believe in a sinless perfection.*

We who accept entire sanctification as a crisis work of grace do believe that even the born again are delivered from a life of sinning. 1 John 3:4— "Whosoever [keeps on committing] sin transgresseth also the law..." The whole idea is that transgression has to be a willful break with God.

We need also to resolve, however, that those of us who are what is called Arminian in doctrine need to clearly know and carefully teach that there is indeed a difference between falling accidentally in, and falling away from, both entrance as well as entire sanctification. Our acceptance of the reality of falling away is not our advocacy of its necessity. The understanding that comes to me is this: some believe that they will not fall away from grace because in the sovereignty of God they cannot. Our underlying belief ought to be that we cannot fall away from grace if in the sufficiency of Christ we will not.

We therefore believe the Bible teaches that,

1. Falling Away from Entrance Sanctification is Only by Transgression

We who accept entrance sanctification as the first crisis work of grace believe that the born again are definitely delivered from a life of sinning (1 John 3:9). We believe this because we understand transgression to be both a willful, deliberate act against a clear commandment of God— "doing on purpose what I know God says is wrong" — and because transgression is also a way of day-to-day acting (1 John 3:4).

In the 1 John 3:9 expression, "doth not commit sin," *commit* is in the present tense and makes the statement to mean, "cannot be sinning as a continuing way of life." Similarly, in 1 John 3:4, *committeth* and *transgresseth* are both in the present tense, and mean "keeping on committing" and "keeping on transgressing." We do not accept, however, that any state of earthly grace, even of entire sanctification, removes us from the possibility of defeat, lapse, error, wrongdoing.

Galatians 6:1— "Brethren, if a man be overtaken in a fault, ye which are spiritual, restore such an one..." The verb tense reveals that "be overtaken" is a one-time act— we may say, an "accident." It does not relate to ongoing activity. There is a difference between successive falling from sustaining some muscle sickness, and a sudden fall from stepping on a slippery melon skin.

So there is a difference between sinful doing as a settled habit and sinful defeat as a single happening. Sometime in your life, since you have come to know God— maybe even since you have been entirely sanctified— you found yourself surprised, overtaken in something which you knew grieved God.

We need to understand, that while both need the blood, a single surprise does not remove you from your work of grace. Too many people have pulled up roots and pulled up roots. What you need to do is go quickly to God and say, "God, I am sorry," and move on your way up the King's Highway.

Peter despicably denied his Lord. He needed and received restoration, but technically he did not need regeneration. In other words, accidental falling is a spiritual tripping. That does, of course, need forgiveness. But accustomed falling is serious transgression that merits forfeiture.

The sum of the matter is that neither sanctification nor perfection rules out becoming. In birthing, burying, and belonging, we have the saintliness to live above transgression or callousness. It is, however, in becoming that we have ongoing strengthening to live above tripping or carelessness. Peter is the classic example (but we are and have our own examples). By a series of lessons in becoming, the man who earlier denied his Lord ended dying for his Lord (John 21:18, 19).

We believe the Bible similarly teaches that,

2. Falling Away from Entire Sanctification is Only by Regression

We who accept entire sanctification as the second crisis work of grace believe that the entirely sanctified are not only definitely delivered from a life of sinning, but also they are decisively delivered from a life of sin or self-sovereignty (Romans 6:6). We believe this because we understand what I am calling regression to be also a willful and deliberate act against committed companionship with God, as well as a way of day-to-day antagonism against redemptive relationship with God (Hebrews 6:4-6).

I am not suggesting that this passage of scripture is confined to the entirely sanctified. I am borrowing it for this context because it so grievously demonstrates deliberateness and repetitious unrighteousness. In Hebrews 6:4, 5, the action related words all represent decided, once-for-all actions. In the Hebrews 6:6a context, the action words "shall fall away" also signify deliberate acts of sin. Further, "fall away" is not a lapse, but a relapse, in its darker meaning. Unequivocally, "fall away" is not an accident but abandonment. In addition, the action words "seeing they crucify to themselves the Son of God afresh, and put him to an open shame" (Hebrews 6:6b) are all in the present tense and also indicate not a sudden shameful accident but a settled regression aversion.

Under the heading of liberation from the saints as lesser suitors, there was reference made to Peter's double behaviour in relation to fellowship with the Gentiles (Galatians 2:11, 12). His conduct was anything but Christlike. The context labels his attitude and action as "dissimulation" (verse 13). It is the word from which comes our English "hypocrisy." It is feigning to be that which one is not. Hypocrisy is the Pharisees' particular sin that Jesus so directly denounced (Luke 12:1). Peter's despicable duplicity was also motivated by dread or a man-fearing spirit (Galatians 2:12b). Further, his dissimulation led even to Barnabas's defilement (Galatians 2:13b).

What was Peter's true spiritual condition? Was he wicked like the Pharisees? The answer must be, No. Then what was his spiritual state? He was guilty of heinous hypocrisy that needed confession and cleansing, but did not necessitate cutting off. We must be courageous to say that while his conduct was marked by great unworthiness, it must have been more a manifestation of weakness than wickedness.

In *My Utmost for His Highest* for September 15, Oswald Chambers is faithful and fearless enough to say, "Envy, jealousy, strife— these things arise not necessarily from the disposition of sin, but from the make-up of our body which was used for this kind of thing in the days gone by." We, too, need to be faithful and fearless enough to teach that there must be a difference between constitutional, chronic carnality (like that of the Corinthians) that induces often falling, and cultural, circumstantial carnality (like that of Peter) that may incite only occasional falling.

The sum of the matter is that neither sanctification nor perfection rules out becoming. In birthing, burying and belonging, we have the saintliness to live above callous regression. It is, however, in becoming that we have ongoing strengthening to live above cultural reverses. Carnal or ingrained unChristlikeness is the presence of badness that requires burying to obliterate.

On the other hand, circumstantial or unguarded unChristlikeness is the absence of balance that requires becoming to overcome. Peter is once more the classic example. By a series of lessons in becoming, and by successive learning, the man who earlier argued about committing himself to the Lord's purification of the Gentiles (Acts 10:9-20) is here not annoyed by, but amenable to and amended by Paul's correction concerning his lapsing, lingering prejudice towards the Gentiles (Galatians 2:14-21).

Becoming is also justified in the light of Theological Truth.

5.2
Theological Truth

THE SCRIPTURES SPEAK OF...

A. The Perfect Law of Liberty

James 1:25— "But whoso looketh into the perfect law of liberty, and continueth therein, he being not a forgetful hearer, but a doer of the work, this man shall be blessed in his deed." The Bible speaks about perfect liberty. If you look into the perfect law of liberty, it seems to me, if there is a perfect law of liberty, we have not only a perfect law, but we can have a perfect liberty. Thank God, the bottom line of walking with God is to get to the place where I am free. That is the whole meaning of liberty.

The perfect law of liberty has to do with the completed scheme of redemption. Perfection is always a process. The Mosaic Law presented redemption in figure only, not in finality (Hebrews 10:1). The perfect law of liberty came, therefore, through process.

This process began, therefore, with what we may call,

1. The Initial Word (Hebrews 1:1)

God revealed divine truth about the Saviour and about

salvation "at sundry times." This truth God did not reveal all at once, but piece by piece.

The process continued and in the fullness of time the law of liberty came to another stage of perfection in,

2. The Incarnate Word (Hebrews 1:2a)

Revelations "in time past" came through many prophets. In complement, but also in contrast, God sent revelation "in these last days" by His one and only begotten Son, the matchless Prince of Peace. He was not words from the Father, but the Word Himself, Who is God (John 1:1). He alone, the incarnate Word, could say, "I am the way, the truth, and the life: no man cometh unto the Father, but by me" (John 14:6).

The contrast of progress in the perfect law of liberty was not only in the one Magnificent Conveyor compared with the many conveyors, but also in the content (John 1:17). Under the New Covenant, God's perfect plan was not the repeated and many symbolical sacrifices required by the Law. Rather, the grace and truth of God's perfect plan was the once-for-all, perfectly sanctifying sacrifice of His Son, the Incarnate Word (Hebrews 10:11, 12, 14). The new content brought by the Incarnate Word includes the revelations of Christ to His apostles. Christ or His Other Comforter revealed unto them so very much that was not known in "other ages." An example of this is Ephesians 3:1-10.

The scheme of redemption has also come to practical perfection in Christians through,

3. The Internalized Word (2 Corinthians 3:3)

David foreshadowed the inwardness of the Word (Psalm 40:8). Generally, however, Old Testament times marked the early periods of the law of liberty, and the truth given by God was particularly external. Basically, the Israelites and others only heard or saw the revelations God made of Himself. The contrast in New Testament times, particularly after the death and resurrection of Christ, is that the truth of God was not only verbally external but also vitally internal.

One mark of the internalized Word is that it became,

a. Internally Engraved (2 Corinthians 3:3)

Figuratively, "heart" refers to the focal point or nerve center of human life or a living person. It represents the inward domain of God's rule. This means that God engraves His laws into our very life and nature. The perfect law of liberty becomes a part of us. The promise of a "new heart" becomes fulfilled in the producing of new creatures (Ezekiel 36:26; 2 Corinthians 5:17).

Another mark of the Internalized Word is that it became,

b. Internally Ingrained (Hebrews 8:10, 16)

Metonymically, "mind" stands for man's function of thinking. It also refers to one's disposition or distinctive manner of thinking and feeling. When God puts and writes His laws in our hearts, the engraved Word creates our new spiritual being. Internally, we become alive to Christ. The impact on our heart is that when He puts and writes His laws in our minds, the Word is now ingrained and characterizes our spiritual thinking and reacting. Internally, we become alert in Christian conscience and Christlike consciousness.

Each Christian ought to maximize this power of scriptural thinking. This power is not so much that of automatic recall as it is of affectionate response. Before the ingraining of the Word there is alienation and enmity towards God (Colossians 1:21). The castaway mind or the carnal mind describes us (Romans 1:28; 8:7).

After the ingraining, there is association and affinity: "and we have known that the Son of God is come, and hath given us a mind, that we may know Him who is true, and we are in Him who is true, in His Son Jesus Christ; this one is the true God..." (1 John 5:20, *Young's Literal Translation*). The mind of Christ now distinguishes us. The power of scriptural thinking is also the power of attentive research.

The ingrained Word is to create a love for the Scriptures. Christians are to do far more than to scan the Scriptures. Like the Berean Christians, the spiritually "well born" are to search the Scriptures (Acts 17:11); that is, they are to scrutinize or to examine them accurately and carefully. It does take the engraved Word, along with the ingrained Word, to search the Scriptures. We may search the Scriptures, but without these possessions we will fail to see the Saviour (John 9:39, 40). The ingrained Word alone gives Christians a confirming mind.

In addition, the power of scriptural thinking is that of approving reason. God's Word and will, embedded in our minds, enable Christians to discern not only between good and bad, but also between better and best (Philippians 1:9, 10). We may say that Christians ought to have a classic mind that serves as a standard of excellence (Romans 12:2).

Christians are neither to be lazy in their use of the Bible nor hazy in their understanding of the Scriptures, for salvation gives them the moral blessing of the engraved Word, and the mental bias of the ingrained Word of God.

The Word is not only engraved and ingrained. The third mark of the internalized Word is that it became,

c. Internally Engrafted (James 1:21b)

The engraved Word creates our new spiritual being (James 1:18). The ingrained Word then characterizes our noble spiritual thinking. Now the engrafted Word conditions our never-ending saintly growing (James 1:21b). There is a work of grace to be done following the first crisis work of God's begetting "us with the word of truth, that we should be a kind of firstfruits of his creatures" (James 1:18b). The Christian is to come to a second crisis of laying apart carnal behaviour and to the steady continuation of increasing in Christlike beauty (James 1:20-27).

The perfect law of liberty that came by the process of becoming proclaims spiritual becoming more significantly than we may immediately realize.

Especially in the light of the glorious liberty of the redemption of the body that is to follow the gracious liberty of the redemption of the soul (Romans 8:21-23; Psalm 49:8; 1 Peter 1:18, 19), there is absolutely no substitute for the birthing, burying, belonging, blessing *and* becoming required by the process of the initial Word, the Incarnate Word and the internalized Word that has led to the perfect law of liberty.

The Scriptures also speak of...

B. Perfect Love (1 John 4:18)

We saw earlier that perfection always involves a process. Because of this, perfect love, like Christian perfection, is not the fittest synonym for entire sanctification. It seems true to say, therefore, that perfect love may not be realized at the moment of entire sanctification.

I must confess that the 1 John 4:18 passage was once a troubling passage to read. I was troubled about the fear I felt when I read that there is no fear in love. I was troubled by the fact that perfect love casts out all fear, and I still had fear. Then I was troubled by the unadorned conclusion that "He that feareth is not made perfect in love." I therefore had triple trouble and double distress! Some Scriptures cause us to bleed, but thanks be to God, others bind us up (Hebrews 4:12-16).

We may consequently suggest three helpful scriptural ways to perfect love. One is,

1. Ended Double-Mindedness (James 1:8)

A double-minded person is a person who has two souls with two different allegiances. Perfect love will elude souls divided in their love interests.

In the early days of my marriage, I did have some little problems other married people don't have. My sweet little girl is like an angel dropped right out of heaven. She has no mischief. She doesn't know how to be mischievous. One of my problems is that I'm chock full of mischief. In fact, I used to look at my pictures and say, *Look at that scamp.* I mean, I am saved and sanctified and in the ministry, but I'd still say, *I see some scampishness in that face.* These days, I'm not seeing it. Maybe I am arriving.

Now, if my wife is a cherub dropped out of heaven, my brother is a double cherub dropped out of heaven. But his little girl is very lively and fun-loving. So whenever we get together I just enjoy myself. One day I had the nerve to say to my brother, who is a really big man, "Don't you think maybe you ought to have married my wife and I ought to have married yours?" My brother pulled himself up to all of his stature and said, "Look here, Wingrove. I don't know whether you have the wrong wife, but I have the right one."

Everyone tells me my little girl is the most wonderful. We were at a business place one day and the lady says, "Do you know that you have a beautiful wife?"

I said, "Yes." She wasn't satisfied. She came back and asked it again. I said, "Yes!"

She must have come back the third time, and then she said, "Do you tell her that you know you have a beautiful wife?" The lady had me under pressure.

I made up my mind that if everybody is telling me I have the most darling and precious wife, I am not going to be left behind. God showed me that you don't fall in love. Love has nothing to do with somebody teasing with you because you're a tease. Love has everything to do

with commitment. If I have committed myself to a cherub, bless her dear heart, I am hers and she is mine, and I do not wish for any other.
Love has nothing to do with the little differences. Love has everything to do with commitment. I thank God for the girl God has given me.
Love for God is not about an emotion. Love for God is not about the feelings He gives you, tickling your ribs. Love for God is about "God, I was made for You. I belong to You, and I am Yours." In the spiritual realm, all of our love belongs all to God, in a way, of course, that cannot be compared even to the best of human marriages. Any double-mindedness in relation to God, any sharing of love for Him makes for spiritual adolescence, if not spiritual adultery (James 4:4). Surrender to God spiritual double-mindedness and He will make an undivided heart an undefiled heart (James 4:8). Purified love lays a firm foundation for the perfecting of love.
Another helpful way to perfect love is,

2. Effective Dwelling

The 1 John 4 passage strongly points to the fact that love, in the first place, is not ours but God's (1 John 4:8, 16). 1 John 4 goes on to indicate that one of the ways that God's love becomes ours is through our dwelling in God and God's dwelling in us (1 John 4:10-12, 16, 17a). Effective dwelling is therefore inter-dwelling. God's fully dwelling in us is contingent upon our dwelling fully in Him (John 15:4, 5). Note that the indwelling of God relates either to the continuing process of the perfecting of love, or to process that has come to completion (1 John 4:12b, 16b, 17a). For the perfecting of love, it is necessary and wonderful for us to live in God and for God to live in us.
The third helpful way to perfect love is,

3. Enlightened Devotion (1 John 2:5-6)

We need to live in the Word and the word; in the Way and the way. The more we look at and live the leadings of God, the more we will love His leadings and progress on the way to perfect love. The sooner, also, will we come to a completion level of that process (1 John 4:16, 17a). I say completion level, because from Zodhiates I understand that we do not have the same perfection level. The level for "each individual," says Zodhiates, differs "according to his God given ability" *(Hebrew Greek Key Study Bible,* p.1761). Each, at individual pace and time, can come to the completed state of the process of perfect love.

I must testify that there are occasional, emotional flashbacks in relation to reading 1 John 4:18. Through ended double-mindedness, effective dwelling and enlightened devotion, however, God has brought me to the delightful place of increasingly restful dwelling in Him. There, fears no longer worry. There, intimate fellowship is more and more wonderful. And there, I no longer question or fear any direction He may give. To His will, my heart no longer says, *Why?* but *Wow!*

Enlightened devotion leads us to an area of never ending becoming. It is this.

The Scriptures that speak of the processes of the perfect law of liberty and of perfect love, also speak of...

C. Progressive Light (Proverbs 4:18)

In practical language Paul verifies the truth of progressive light. 1 Corinthians 13:11 — "When I was a child, I spake as a child, I understood as a child, I thought as a child: but when I became a man, I put away childish things." We are learning, learning, learning. I can see, as I look back over my life, that the light has come, maybe slower than I would wish, but it has come. And it has kept coming. And thanks be unto God, He has brought me to a place where I have never been at such rest in

God. Light! That is why, more and more, I get into the Word of God. I want to know what God says.

There obviously is a crisis letting go of ourselves to God and a crisis sanctification (John 12:24; Ephesians 5:25, 26). Someone shared with me a statement that he said my preacher brother made. The substance is this: "When— in the light of all that we know about self— we have surrendered ourselves to God— in the light of all we know about God— that is holiness" (crisis). As we grow in holiness, however, there is more and more light to get about God, ourselves and life, and more and more light to walk in (1 John 1:7). Since light and knowledge increase as we grow in God, then better and fuller understanding call for continual becoming. The more we see of the glory of the Lord, the more we are to be changed into the glory of His Christlikeness (2 Corinthians 3:18).

Let me once more testify. In my Christian experience, I had birthing in 1947. Three years later, in 1950, I came to the crisis blessing of being filled with the Spirit. It was during the God's Bible School and College mid-winter revival. The blessing was without demonstration, but it was definite and dynamic. There I place my crisis victory of entire sanctification.

About 1959, however— some nine years following— truth about burying came clear and searching. After some hesitation, I fully walked in the light.

About 1968— after the passage of another nine years— God helped me to come to grips with becoming. I began walking in the light.

Since 1992, truth about belonging has been exploding in my soul. More than ever I am walking in the light. More than ever I know and love the preciousness and purity of holiness vision and victory. Light continues to come of clarifications and better understanding of how holiness works in all of the areas of life.

For example, it is not difficult to forgive others and

myself, when I see that the foundation of forgiveness is not ours but God's (Daniel 9:9a).

I will not try to analyze my complex, back-and-forth, roundabout journey to the spiritual plane on which God has helped me to stand today. Three lessons seem to emerge, however. We very likely need clearer teaching in holiness. Following definite experiences in entire sanctification there is light to walk in. As we walk in the light we do not need continually to multiply altars of groundwork crises, but we need constantly to mount altars of growing conformity.

The biblical truths of the perfect law of liberty, of perfect love, and of progressive light declare the necessity of becoming. The crisis-emphasizing circle of holiness believers need more and more to teach and practice becoming as a vital heartbeat of holiness.

To add to the theological understanding of perfection and transgression, and to the biblical truth of perfect liberty, perfect love, and progressive light, the Bible reinforces the reality and need of becoming with Practical Truth.

5.3
Practical Truth

ONE STEP IN BIBLICAL, practical becoming is —

A. Exposure

2 Corinthians 3:18— "But we all, with open face beholding as in a glass the glory of the Lord, are changed into the same image from glory to glory, even as by the Spirit of the Lord." "With open face beholding as in a glass" is the language of exposure.

This openness speaks of,

1. Nakedness before God's Enlightening

No veils are to cover our faces, our whole being, as Moses covered his face so that Israel was not blinded by the fullness of glory nor bewildered by the fading of the glory (2 Corinthians 3:13). There is to be no trying to hide who or what we truly are from God, from ourselves, or from others. There is to be no fear of what may be found. We are to erase the word "embarrassment" from our spiritual vocabulary. We are not divine. We are human. We have imperfections. We may fail and make mistakes. We are to be wide and unashamedly open to all of God's fullness and findings.

The "face" conveys the idea of,

2. Nearness to God's Eye

"Face" means near to the eye. It represents anyone or anything turned or presented to the eye of another. It is the nearest and most direct presence. It is eyes that are not inclined downward. It is eye-to-eye contact. It is one's face that is towards God, not one's side, not one's back. It is not an Adam hiding from God or a Jonah trying to get away from the presence of the Lord. It is both the openness and the nearness that speak of cooperating with God's seeing and His scrutinizing.

"Beholding as in a glass the glory of the Lord," emphasizes,

3. Noting God's Excellence

Some commentators say that "beholding as in a glass" means reflecting as a glass. Looking in a glass or mirror seems to fit the context better. At this point, we do the looking. The reflecting comes later.

Some say the glass represents the written Word of God. There is warrant for this (James 1:22-25). The Bible is a marvelous mirror. The Psalmist tells us how wonderful is the mirror of God's Word (Psalm 19:7-9).

The glass could also represent the Living Word, Jesus Himself, for it is in Him that we see, in person, God's glory (2 Corinthians 4:6). With the Greeks, we would see Jesus (John 12:20, 21). With Peter, James, and John we would, in fact, see no one save Jesus only (Mark 9:8). In the glass we see "the glory of the Lord." Glory is splendour, brightness, magnificence, adornment, preeminence, honour, renown.

All of this and more we surely see in the written Word, but especially in Jesus, the living Word. There is so much to see. Are we beholding? Are we fully open and exposing ourselves to God?

Dr. Vernon McGee used Nathaniel Hawthorne's story about a village where there was a rock formation, and part of the formation was a stone face. Legend had it that, someday, somebody with the same kind of face would come to the village and it would be a means of great blessing. That story took hold of a little boy and he gazed long at the stone face.

The years passed by. He became a young man, then he became an old man. One day, he was tottering down the street. Somebody looked up and saw him coming and shouted, "He has come! The one who looks like the great stone face is here." The little boy had looked so long— through all of his life, into manhood, into old age, looking at the stone face— that now he looked like the stone face.

Of course, it's just a story. But when we keep looking at Jesus, we become like Him. These days, when I am tempted to look at people, I feel a little tap on my shoulder: *Look at Me, Wingrove.* When I find a temptation to criticize, God is right there saying, *Look at Me.*

This illustration is a good introduction of the truth that we are to do more than ensure exposure. Practical becoming also calls for...

B. Exchange (2 Corinthians 3:18b)

The Greek word for "changed" is one from which we get our English word "metamorphosis." It is not a superficial change, but a substantial change. It is not a casual or merely external change, like being conformed to the world (Romans 12:2). It is concrete and internal, like a caterpillar becoming a butterfly. It "refers to the permanent state to which a change takes place."

Besides here in 2 Corinthians, there are only three other scriptural passages that carry this word, "changed." It is "transformed" (Romans 12:2), and "transfigured" (Matthew 17:2; Mark 9:2). (Interestingly, all the twos.) We may characterize the expressions in this way: In transform there is exchange for the better. In transfigure it is exchange for the blazing; while in the Corinthian passage— which we may call transfuse (diffuse or scatter through)— it is exchange for the beautiful. This not a superficial, cosmetic change but a substantial, character change.

One evidence of entire sanctification is that the possessors of it not only have a commitment to change, but also they do change. Very naturally, one of my mottos in these days is, "Committed to change." I am committed to the big changes as well as the smaller. The entirely sanctified are to be committed to change.

Added to exposure and exchange, we now consider one other very important practical aid to becoming. It is...

C. Exercise

The Bible presents two means or methods of exercise. One is related to,

1. Punishment for Spiritual Athletes (Hebrews 12:5-11)

Jesus says, *I am the Coach, and I have to deal with you; I have to punish you; I have to chastise you sometimes.* It may take the form of correction with words ("chasteneth," verse 6a); or of chastisement by whippings ("scourgeth," verse 6b). We may be enraged by the punishments which God gives— defying them (holding them in contempt), or enervated by them— that is, becoming discouraged, downhearted, depressed, or even despairing (Hebrews 12:5). We ought, instead, to be "exercised" by them (Hebrews 12:11).

We are exercised by divine punishments when we accept them as coming from God; when we cooperate with all of God's purposes during the punishment; when we learn the lessons God would teach us; and when we gain the lasting benefits God would give us. The appropriate response to the exercise of divine punishment is therefore, "Spanks, thanks"; then learn the hard lesson from some bad failure, and move forward spiritually with greater victory.

Hurricane Marilyn blew away the house I was staying in. I went to an island on Thursday, preached Thursday night, and the hurricane came on Friday. No more preaching; I needed to get out on Monday for another appointment. The airport was damaged.

There was devastation everywhere, and I'm saying, "I must get out on Monday. I must get out on Monday." It was a voice of faith, really.

People laughed at me. "Why don't you stop that nonsense?"

Sunday night we were in this home where I had been rescued, and there was a knock at the door. It happened that the manager of Federal Express— who had come by helicopter into the island, and brought a relative of this family— was at the door. Immediately, my heart began to bubble. *The manager of Federal Express! These people deal with planes!*

I said to him, "Sir, this is my situation. I need to get out of here tomorrow."

The man says, "No problem. I will arrange it."

He is now leaving the house, and I say to him, "Sir, you don't know how much like Santa Claus you look to me." Immediately, there were spanks like fire. I could feel the strap of God. I have never been in so much hot water.

I said, *Wingrove, you say you believe in God, but you are nothing more than a downright, deluded, deceived hypocrite! God sends rescue to your door and as quickly as that, you call God, Santa Claus?* I was in real trouble.

First thing I did was to confess. We were having a little prayer meeting before bedtime, and I said, "I've got something to say. I'm terribly sorry, but this is what I said..." Some people felt I didn't even need to make that confession, but I made it, anyway.

Next morning I got up early. Six o'clock... Seven o'clock... no Santa Claus. Nine o'clock, no Santa Claus. And finally I say, *Yes, I understand, God. I understand I blew it. I understand that I deserve what I'm getting. I understand. I'm going to try to get to a telephone and I will tell the people I cannot come.*

The voice was as clear and as soft as could be: *I want you to know that I am not a vindictive God. You let me down last night, but I will not let you down today.*

It was the first time in my life that I knew that my God was not a vindictive God.

Would you believe, by twelve o'clock God got me out of St. Thomas (without Santa Claus). I could almost say, *God, I thank you I made that mistake, because I learned out of that, that You are not a vindictive God.*

God showed me that one of the reasons why I am in such trouble when I fail Him, is not so much that I let God down, but I let myself down. We have such a standard that we put, that we can't get over the fact that we let ourselves down. God says, *Look up here. I am the great big God Who will punish you to bless you.*

We are now doing some active grandparenting. We have a little three-year-old. He is sharp of eye, sharp of muscle, he is quick.

This day he had an object that he shouldn't have. It was very important, very precious. When I saw him with it, I reached out to get it. The boy saw my movement, pulled away, and I pulled again. He pulled away. Next thing you know, a seventy-six-year-old grandfather was in a grabbing contest with a three-year-old boy. I mean, the boy gave me a run for my money, as they say.

I have to exert strength, and finally, I got the thing. And when I got it, I kind of growled, "Give me that!"

And I could see God, looking down, and saying, *What a sight*. It was the first time in my life that I felt chastised, but I did not feel condemned.

What God showed me is that isn't my habit. I'm not flying off the handle every other day. If that had happened to me some years ago, I would say, *Oh, dear! Oh, dear! I thought... I thought... I thought... I thought I was on the mountain. Now I'm not*. That was no carnal behaviour; it was stupid behaviour.

God says, *Next time, don't begin the grabbing game*.

The other means or method of exercise is related to,

2. Practice by Spiritual Athletes.

1 Timothy 4:7 — "...exercise thyself rather unto godliness."

"Exercise," here, as in that from the punishment of spiritual children, is the most strenuous, vigorous, and unhindered gymnastic activity. It is also formal and full training that takes place in a school of athletics. It is important to note that while the punishment type of exercise is occasional and then over, the practice type of exercise is to be continual and ongoing.

We need to understand, value, and profitably use situations that tempt us to unkindness, impatience, jealousy, envy, boasting, pride, haughtiness, selfishness, rudeness, self-will, irritability, harshness, anger, touchiness, malice, retaliation. These are really wonderful opportunities to practice becoming proficient and prolific in producing the fruit of the Spirit, and in portraying the beauty of holiness.

God uses the exercise of punishment for spiritual athletes and practice for spiritual athletes. 1 Timothy 4:7 — "...exercise thyself... unto godliness."

Exercise yourself! Every time God puts you in a situation where you can get angry, that's a chance to say, *Thank You, God. It's a chance for me to practice not being angry*.

Jealous? *Thank You, God. It's a chance for me to practice not being jealous.*

Or *Thank You, God. It's a chance for me to practice not being in a grabbing game. Thank You, God,* and I keep practicing and practicing and practicing.

A lot of us have so emphasized crisis that we are in a lot of crisis. We need to look at the whole picture of holiness.

5.4
Conclusion

CHRISTIAN CERTAINTY HAS BEEN deepening. Conformity to Christ has been increasing. I am a firm believer in Becoming. Paradoxical truth requires it. Theological truth reveals it. Practical truth reinforces it.

Holiness is the darling doctrine of the Church. It is universal. It is God's requirement for all. It is exceedingly practical and wonderful. It is all about finding God to live in us by faith in God alone. It is all about facilitating God to labour in and through us by falling before Him and Him alone. The secret of living and loving the life of holiness, and leading others to it, is to have the healthy holiness of Birthing, Burying, Belonging, Blessing and Becoming. There is victory for whoever will walk in this glorious light of holiness!

MEMBERS OF SCHMUL'S WESLEYAN BOOK CLUB
BUY THESE OUTSTANDING BOOKS AT 40% OFF
THE RETAIL PRICE

Join Schmul's Wesleyan Book Club by calling toll-free:
800-S$_7$P$_7$B$_2$O$_6$O$_6$K$_5$S$_7$

Put a discount Christian bookstore in your own mailbox

Visit us on the Internet at
www.wesleyanbooks.com

Schmul Publishing Company | PO Box 776 | Nicholasville, KY 40340

www.ingramcontent.com/pod-product-compliance
Lightning Source LLC
LaVergne TN
LVHW052257070426
835507LV00036B/3240